Manchester **EveningNews** WEEKEND

Family Walks Guide 2nd Edition

A guide to another 45 easy walks
based on the popular
Manchester Evening News
Saturday column

By John & Anne Nuttall

Front cover photos: Bolton Abbey, Wharfedale
Packet House & Bridgewater Canal, Worsley

diversemedia

Acknowledgements

Published by Diverse Media Ltd, 164 Deansgate, Manchester M60 2RD
Tel: 0161-211 2633; fax: 0161-839 1488; e-mail: citylife@mcr-evening-news.co.uk;
website: www.manchesteronline.co.uk

Managing Editor: Mike Hill
Designer: Robert Langley
Text & Photos: John & Anne Nuttall ©
Maps: Dick Graham, Gill Craig, Simon Thorley
Front and back cover photographs: John Nuttall ©

With special thanks to: Eric Jackson, Gill Craig & Peter Devine,
the Diverse Media marketing team, and the Manchester Evening News colour room.

Published in **October 1999**.
Printed and Bound by MFP Design and Print, Manchester.

ISBN: 095290869-7

Contents

The Old Hall, Prestbury

Foreword

To say that the Nuttalls are nutty about walking would be an understatement: a bit like saying Sir Alex Ferguson has a passing interest in Manchester United. Congleton husband-and-wife team John and Anne must have covered more ground in the north west than any other couple. What they don't know about our wonderful and varied terrain you could fit on the back of a postage stamp.

Their authoritative walking columns, complete with photos and detailed maps, in the *Manchester Evening News* Weekend Go section have turned them into our very own Wainwrights... the definitive voice of rambling for the '90s and beyond. But the beauty of the Nuttalls' approach is that they are not countryside purists. They are just as at home writing about some brilliant trail through the green fringes of Didsbury or Castlefield as they are about celebrated walks in the Lakes or Peak District.

Go on one of their walks any weekend and look around at some of the other walkers. Notice how many of them are holding torn out walks pages from the *MEN*, or better still, clutching a book compiled from those pages. Take my word for it, there'll be loads of them. And if you're lucky, you may even see Anne in her famous pink anorak or John taking photographs.

But at the *MEN* we don't believe that you can have too much of a good thing, so we've decided to offer this second *Family Walks Guide* edition, featuring 45 wonderful rambles from north, south, east and west of the region that have appeared in the paper.

There's something for everyone, from the wild beauty of the Goyt Valley to the bracing seascape of Formby, from the genteel pastures of Prestbury to the hidden gems of Worsley. Which means that wherever you live, there's a great walk virtually on your doorstep, but definitely not through your garden - the Nuttalls always get the route right! That's because they do them all personally, and don't lift them out of other books like some writers.

In the years they've been working for the *Manchester Evening News*, I've only ever had one complaint about their walks, from someone who couldn't get through a canal tunnel. As it happened, the tunnel had been blocked off by the local water company to carry out maintenance a day after the walk appeared in the paper.

So, still a 100% unblemished record for our team who, to use soccer parlance, never give less than 110% in providing walking excellence. Enjoy.

Eric Jackson

Weekend Go editor

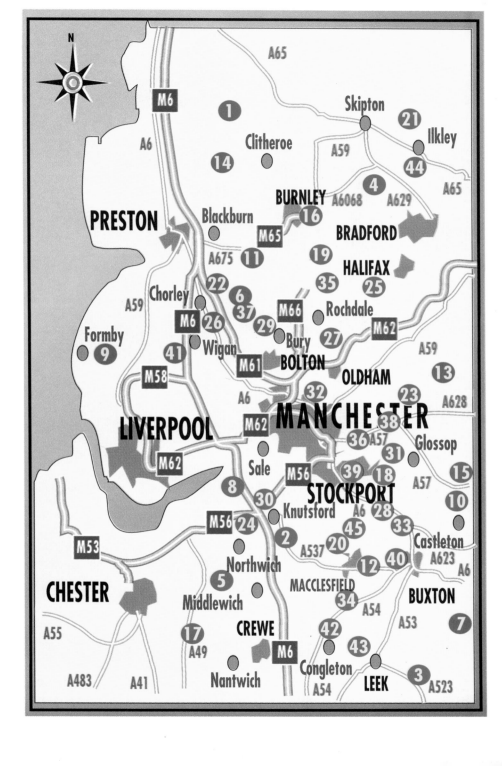

CAN YOU HANDLE THE SUSPENSE?

Newton

LOCATION: Forest of Bowland

START: Dunsop Bridge, 8 miles north west of Clitheroe.
Car park, toilets

DISTANCE: 7 miles

GRADE: Moderate

BUS: From Clitheroe: 110 & 111;
Summer Suns: 40

TIME: 3½ hours

MAP: Outdoor Leisure - Forest of Bowland, Landranger 103

REFRESHMENTS: Parkers Arms

Dominated by the high fells of the Forest of Bowland, Dunsop Bridge is the village closest to the centre of Britain. Yet despite its fame, there were remarkably few people about as we followed the ancient paths and tracks across the fields. Peewits swooped and called, and swallows skimmed low in search of insects: then, as we reached a limestone stile, a stoat froze motionless and stared at us in disbelief. We were probably the first people it had seen all week. But the high spot of the walk is the Heath Robinson suspension bridge over the River Hodder. Here, as it bounces and sways, you cross one at a time - definitely a walk to remember.

THE ROUTE

Just before the bridge in the centre of the village, turn right along the Private Road. The tarmac ends at Holme Head Cottages, and nearing the footbridge you turn right up a steep bluebell-covered bank. The powerline is then a useful guide across the field to Beatrix, a hamlet dating back to the Norman Conquest and once a major marketplace.

Follow the road past the houses and, going through the leftmost gate, the track climbs gently, with extensive views over the Hodder Valley. Reaching an old hedgerow, the right of way short-cuts left across pathless grass to Back of the Hill Barn, then veers left downhill to Oxenhurst Clough.

Now an obvious grassy track leads up past Rough Syke Barn to a gate on the skyline, and at the gate beyond, you join Bull Lane, the highest point of the walk, with a fine view of the Forest of Bowland. Follow the track, then at the second bend keep straight on through a small gate and across the shakehole-pitted field to Gamble Hole Farm. This was the birthplace in 1731 of Robert Parker, the Halifax lawyer who broke up the infamous Crag Coiners Gang.

Passing to the left of the buildings, go right in the field beside the wall, then at the corner take the leftmost gate, and head diagonally to a stile onto the road. Continuing straight over, you descend to a stream full of the blue-flowered brooklime and follow the hedge round to the right, heading for a stile by a barn. Stiles then lead down over the fields to Newton.

Entering the village, which has many lovely old houses, keep straight on, down past the Georgian Parkers Arms, to cross Newton Bridge. The River Hodder is then followed downstream until, after the second stile, you climb across the fields through a couple of gates to join a lane by a barn.

Turn right to pass the 16th century Foulscales with its mullioned windows. The little bump on the side is the 'garderobe', a medieval lavatory. Just after the barns, take the Private Road, then in about 300 yards a footpath leads across the fields to the suspension bridge which swings alarmingly as you cross.

Reaching the safety of the far side, aim to the right of

River Dunsop

Knoll Wood where a path leads out to the road. Turn left and then, immediately after Boarsden, a footpath sign points into a cobbled yard. Exiting through a garden gate, a track leads down towards the river, and past another suspension bridge to a footbridge. Here the pointed Sugar Loaf Hill, once the site for a gibbet, can be seen to the right, and ahead is a gleaming white aqueduct. Though there is no sign of a path, continue by the river and through a little wood, thick with garlic-scented ramsons, then crossing the field to Thorneyholme Hall Bridge, you turn right to the village.

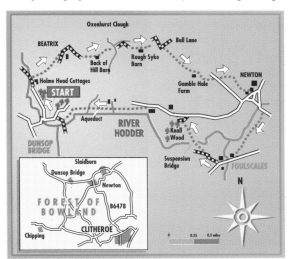

CHESHIRE'S RURAL PAST

Gargoyle, Peover Church

LOCATION: South of Knutsford

START: Lay-by on A50, two miles from Knutsford.

DISTANCE: 5½ miles

GRADE: Easy

TIME: 3 hours

NOTE: Peover Hall & Gardens open from May, Mon 2pm-5pm (closed BH). Gardens only, Thu 2pm-5pm

BUS: Between Knutsford & Macclesfield 26 & 27 Not Sun

MAP: Pathfinder 758, Landranger 118

REFRESHMENTS: Whipping Stocks Inn

Walking down leafy lanes and across the open parkland of Peover Hall, where cows seem mildly surprised by strangers, you feel you have stepped back in time. This is a Cheshire landscape from a more leisurely age, when Manchester was half a day away, and London a three day's journey by stage coach. Pronounced Peever, the name comes from the river, meaning 'the bright one'. And it is certainly appropriate, for in early summer the hedgerows and verges are bright with flowers, while azaleas and rhododendrons surround the hall in a patchwork of colour.

THE ROUTE

Turning your back on Knutsford, follow the A50 then, opposite the whitewashed Ridge Cottage, turn left on the track. Flanked by arable fields, this leads past a half-timbered house, and continues as a footpath. Radbroke Hall, the home of Barclay's Bank, can be seen above the trees, while ahead, on the distant horizon, is the flat-topped peak of Shutlingsloe.

At the path junction in the middle of the field, keep straight on, until reaching a little footbridge you cross a newly landscaped field. Passing a pond, turn right to follow the grassy ride beside the hedge until, approaching the tarmac track, you cross a stile and continue on the far side of the hedge to Stocks Lane.

Turn right along the road past Radbroke Hall to the Whipping Stocks Inn, once a halt for stage coaches on their way to London, then crossing the road to the white lodge gates you enter Peover Park. An avenue of horse chestnuts leads to a cattle grid by a lake, then the right of way forks right. Now Peover Hall comes into view, a rather angular red brick structure built in 1585.

When the track diverges from the fence, cross the stile and continue by the fence, with views of the immaculate topiary. Turning left over a way-marked stile, you come to an incongruous short section of wall, a memorial stile erected by the present owner. The path

10

then enters the trees, and as it weaves through the rhododendrons and past a 500-year-old oak, there are tantalising glimpses of the private gardens.

A narrow walk of hornbeams, their branches trained rigidly to attention, brings you to Peover Church, a mixture of brick and gritstone dating from 1450, with some interesting gargoyles. Passing an ornamental sundial, you follow the cobbles round the stable block and out to a road junction.

Peover Park

Turn right along Long Lane until, passing St Anthony's Cottage, the bridleway becomes unsurfaced, while flanking fields grow dandelions and setaside grants. Lime trees edge the partly cobbled quiet track, and the lane continues by acres of glasshouses and on past Longlane Farm.

Crossing the busy A50 to a stile, a footpath leads across the fields to the right of Peover Old Farm and then bears left to join Free Green Lane. This quiet little country road, which acquired its name because it ran through common land, is followed past Cheers Green Farm which was built in 1720.

Continue straight on past Middle Lane, then after the cottages a bridleway forks right into the trees to pass in front of Freegreen Farm, with its unusual square turrets. Going through the farmyard, Sandy Lane continues across the fields, until reaching the A50 you turn left back to the lay-by.

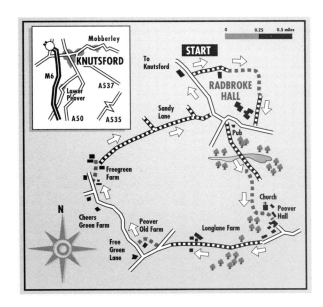

THOR'S WAYS ARE MANIFOLD

Thor's Cave

LOCATION: 10 miles south of Buxton

START: Wettonmill car park

(Grid reference 095561), toilets

DISTANCE: 3½ miles

GRADE: Moderate

TIME: 2 hours

MAP: Outdoor Leisure - White Peak, Landranger 119

REFRESHMENTS: Royal Oak & Wetton Mill

High above the Manifold Valley on a vertical wall of limestone rock stands Thor's Cave, the fabled home of the Thunder God. Once Palaeolithic hunters lived under its great roof and, from the safety of its shelter, watched wolves, bears and woolly rhinoceros in the valley below. Yet though the cave was formed millions of years ago by water cutting down through the rock, the River Manifold itself is an enigma. There is plenty of water at Wettonmill, but here you can stand among the whitened stones of the dry river bed, for the Manifold has gone, vanished down fissures into an unknown world of caverns far beneath your feet.

THE ROUTE

From Wettonmill (an ancient corn mill first mentioned in 1577), follow the lower road down the valley. This was the track of the Manifold Light Railway which was built in 1904, but it lasted barely 30 years for 'it starts from nowhere and ends up at the same place'.

As the old railway continues over a bridge, traffic is barred and the only hazard is cyclists. Rounding the bend, Ossam's Crag appears, an impressive wall of limestone traversed by the overhangs of Cummerbund, one of the valley's excellent rock climbs. Then Thor's Cave comes into view: with its splendid mountainous shape, the crag is a tempting objective, but the huge and mysterious black cave mouth is irresistible. A footbridge spans the river, usually dry except in winter, and the path enters the trees.

Enthusiastic feet have scoured a path directly up the hillside, but it is easier to take the left-hand branch. Reaching a signpost, you turn right up a few steps to traverse the slope through coppiced hazel until, as the direct route is rejoined, the path begins to climb in earnest. But it is only a short effort, and soon the cave is reached. At close hand, it looks even more impressive, but a scramble up inside - very slippery if wet - yields the finest view with the hillside framed in a black silhouette. Excavated in 1864, the finds can be seen in Buxton Museum.

Now the route goes leftwards, a clear path round the hillside to a stile. After descending into a dip, you climb beside the wall to a stile at the top of the field, where a track is joined. A couple of tortoiseshell butterflies danced ahead of us as we walked out to the road and turned right into Wetton Village, a settlement dating back to the 7th century. Continuing past the church, go left at the bend, but if you're feeling thirsty the Royal Oak is down to the right.

Follow the road uphill and carry straight on through the squeezer stile, then going through another squeezer, where fossils are revealed in the polished rock, you enter National Trust land. Keep straight on across the grassy hillslope and down to a stile in the fence. The next field is crossed diagonally, then staying on the right of the wall you follow it into the valley at Pepper Inn.

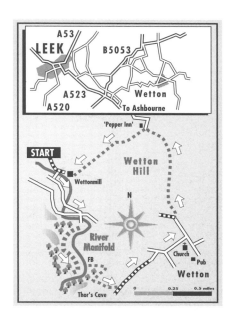

Now a private house, this was an isolation hospital during a smallpox outbreak among the workmen building the Manifold Railway.

Turn left through the gate and follow the stream down, then as the valley bends left you take the path which climbs to a little wooden gate. Crossing the grassy ridge go right, towards Wettonmill, but before a welcome cup of tea at the cafe, walk across to Nan Tor, for exploring its caves makes a fitting end to the walk.

Ossams Crag

13

WYCOLLER WUZZIN HOLES

LOCATION: Near Colne

START: One mile east of Trawden car park

DISTANCE: 3 miles

GRADE: Easy, but with a short, steep ascent

TIME: 1½ hours

NOTE: Information Centre open most weekends, toilets

BUS: X43 to Laneshaw Bridge

MAP: Outdoor Leisure - South Pennines, Landranger 103

REFRESHMENTS: Wycoller

Fireplace in the ruins of Wycoller Hall

The picturesque hamlet of Wycoller, near Colne, looks as if it has stepped straight out of a picture book. Gritstone cottages, their gardens full of flowers, cluster round an ancient pack-horse bridge; close by are the gaunt ruins of Wycoller Hall, while the beck is crossed by no fewer than seven bridges, each with a different character. Wycoller has changed little since the 19th century and a climb to Viewpoint Rocks is rewarded by a bird's eye view of the pastoral valley. But there is a wildness about the surrounding moors, for this is Brontë country. Here Charlotte once walked, high above Wycoller Dean, and saw where Jane Eyre and Mr Rochester could be united at last.

THE ROUTE

Traffic is restricted to preserve Wycoller's tranquillity, so from the car park follow the footpath beside the road. Joining the tarmac, where upright stone slabs, known as Vaccary Walling, date back to the 12th century, it is then only a few yards down into the village.

Crossing Laithe Hill Bridge, follow the road round to the right beside the little stream. In the 18th century, the main occupation of Wycoller changed from agriculture to handloom weaving and in the walls of Pierson's House are 'wuzzin holes' where wet yarn was 'wuzzed' round in a basket to dry. Passing the Craft Centre, you come to the twin-arched packhorse bridge which leans somewhat precariously over the beck. The next bridge is an 18th century clapper bridge, constructed from huge stone slabs.

Continue by the ruined Wycoller Hall, the inspiration for Ferndean Manor in Jane Eyre, and beyond is the 1630s Aisled Barn, now an Information Centre. After the picnic area, you reach Copy House Bridge and cross to a little gated stile. It is then a short, but steep climb beside the wall to join a track where you turn left. Passing Copy House, follow the old walled lane, which continues to climb, then just before you reach the gate, turn left on a narrow path along the top of the hillslope.

14

Packhorse Bridge

Raven Rock Farm, to the right, was named after the massive rock beside it, and the path leads through newly planted woodland and across a moor of bilberry and gritstone boulders. Keeping high above the valley, continue through a couple of small wooden gates to a ladder stile into a field. Turn right and follow the wall round to a gate into the next field, then go left and across the adjacent field to a wooden stepstile.

Arriving at the gritstone outcrop of Viewpoint Rocks, there are views of the long ridge of Boulsworth Hill, and you look across to Foster's Leap, named after Foster Cunliffe from Wycoller Hall, who jumped between two of the rocks for a bet.

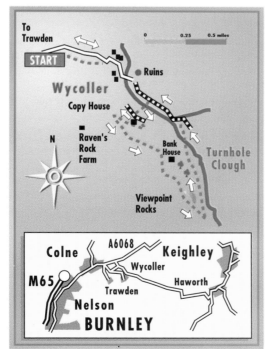

Descending slightly to a ladder stile at the wall junction, follow the wall until just before a gate onto the open hillside, you double back down the secluded moorland valley. The path goes over a stile by the stream and follows the fence above Turnhole Clough, newly planted with wild cherry, silver birch, rowan and beech.

Entering the trees, the path continues past a footbridge to go left over a stile, then follows the fence along a flagged path below Bank House. The stream is crossed at a second footbridge, and joining the valley track, you pass Clam Bridge. The single gritstone slab has small holes on one side for a hand rail, and is believed to be over 1000 years old. It is now an easy stroll back down Wycoller Dean to Wycoller.

15

SALT OF THE EARTH

LOCATION: 5 miles south west of Northwich

START: Whitegate Way car park
(Grid reference 615680), toilets

DISTANCE: 6 (or 4½) miles

GRADE: Easy

TIME: 2 to 3 hours

MAP: Pathfinder 775 and a tiny bit of 758,
Landranger 118

REFRESHMENTS: Pack a flask

Churchill Wood

The heady, almond scent of golden gorse hung in the air, and mallards landed with a flurry and splash, as we walked beside the lakes of Newchurch Common. This is the heart of Cheshire's salt region, where once chasms appeared overnight as the ground, and sometimes houses too, collapsed into the workings. But though salt and sand quarrying have shaped the countryside, nature has reclaimed the land, and now the disused quarries form attractive open water. Horses and walkers follow an old railway built to carry salt, and thrushes sing in woods that seem little changed by the centuries.

THE ROUTE

From the car park follow the Whitegate Way behind the Victorian station and under the bridge, where boxes provide a refuge for bats. Soon walkers and horses are segregated and the line, which closed in 1966, leads past fields and exclusive houses. After about a mile, you turn right onto Newchurch Common and go left round the lake. Formed by sand quarrying, the lake with its fringe of gorse, silver birch and Scots pine is now a popular home for the great crested grebe.

Reaching a track (the line of an old mineral railway), you turn left, then in about 300 yards, a footpath goes right, above the lake beside the holly hedge. Emerging onto a track, continue through the farmyard and along the lane where Daleford Manor hides behind a tall brick wall, and out to the road.

Go straight across through the trees into the field, and continue beside the fence past a playground for traffic cones, a police skid-pan. A yellow way-mark is welcome reassurance, then the path goes left for a few yards before entering Pettypool Wood at a stile. Keeping straight on, you walk beneath tall larch trees, rowan and weeping silver birch, while to the left is the Cheshire Forest guide camp.

Negotiating a fallen tree-trunk, the path continues through rhododendrons and beside a brook until, at a signpost, you go right across a bridge and up to join a forest track. The Short Route turns right here and follows the track back to the road.

Turning left, the track comes to Petty Pool with its water-lilies and spear-like iris leaves, and continues beside it. At the edge of the wood, you cross the field, and follow the fence of Keeper's Cottage to emerge onto a farm track. Go left, then just past the house, a stile on the right leads to a stream and a boardwalk constructed by conservation volunteers.

The path continues through the trees, where bright marsh marigolds bloom in the spring, and at a stile you turn right into Churchill Wood, protected as an SSSI. A stone causeway leads through the swamps where marsh horsetail and broad buckler fern grow beneath the alder trees, then a way-mark points right and the path climbs to join a track. Fork right across a dip to a forest track and, turning right again, you walk through the pines of Sherratts Rough.

Reaching the road, turn right: then, as the pavement comes to an end, you

Newchurch Common

meet the Short Route and turn left down Lapwing Hall Farm drive. In 100 yards, a path goes right over a stile then although the right of way goes diagonally across the field, most people follow the edge. At a step stile, the path leads through the narrow belt of trees and across the track. Continue on the sandy path beyond to the Whitegate Way, where you turn left back to the old station.

17

A TURN ON TURTON

By the ruins of Whewell's Farm

LOCATION: 7 miles north of Bolton
START: Crookfield Road Car Park on A675
DISTANCE: 6 miles
GRADE: Moderate
TIME: 3 hours
NOTES: Some pathless walking, but no problems in clear weather. Boots and compass recommended
MAP: Explorer - West Pennine Moors, Landranger 109
REFRESHMENTS: Pack a flask

It was hot, there was no-one about and high above Belmont only a few black-faced sheep moved on Turton Moor. Here tumbled stones are a reminder of vanished upland farms, while purple moor-grass and the stiff wiry stems of mat-grass stretch as far as the eye can see. But in front of us a pied wagtail alighted on the wall, curlews with their long curved beaks soared in the breeze, while circling anxiously, a peewit called insistently to lure us away from its nest. Then as we walked on across the moor, the larks kept up a continuous song and meadow pipits, with their characteristic dipping flight, dropped camouflaged into the grass.

THE ROUTE

From the road corner beyond the picnic area, a public footpath sign points the way along a track. Soft rush smothers the rough grazing and, in the ditch, the ivy-leaved water-crowfoot flowers all summer. Winter Hill is easily identified by its array of masts, then passing the gaunt, white-painted ruins of Lower Pasture Barn, Belmont Reservoir, which was built in 1826, appears ahead.

Ignoring the turning to the farms below, you continue round the hillside, with distant views of Bolton, then a sign to Turton Moor points left, but with no path it is easier to continue another 200 yards and take the clear grassy track across the moor.

Beyond the ruins of Moor Side, the next section is pathless, so heading north-east, past a temporary survey mast for a thankfully now abandoned windfarm, in a quarter mile you join the line of an old tramway. Follow this for about 100 yards and then fork left on a narrow path which brings you to a nameless high-walled ruin.

A faint path, heading just south of east, leads towards an ancient windswept hawthorn hedge, then reaching the first tree, a narrow trod leads off left. Though now just wild moorland, this was the site of Turton Moor Colliery, which only closed in the 1920s.

A pile of stacked slates marks another abandoned farm, and the indistinct path keeps a level course above a rush-filled ditch. Reaching a stile, aim for the solitary tree beside the remains of Whewell's Farm, where the original stone-lined wells can still be found. Commuting to work is no modern phenomenon for this was the home of George Whewell, the local executioner, and in 1651 during the Civil War he had to travel to Bolton to behead the Earl of Derby.

Continuing round the hillside a rough track is joined at a signpost, and turning left you climb gently, heading for another colliery, which closed around 1870. But 200 yards after passing a solitary stone gatepost, fork right to descend to a feeder stream for the Bradshaw Brook reservoirs. Crossing the wooden bridge, you climb past the ruins of Green Lowe and turn left on the track.

On reaching a little waterfall,

By the feeder stream

the track veers left back towards the stream, and this acts as a guide up onto the moor. A cairn with a big wooden post stands beside more old mine workings, while to the north lies Darwen Moor, the scene of a mass trespass in 1878 which started an 18 year fight to regain open access.

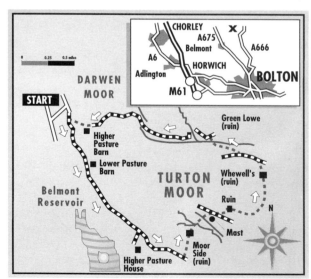

At a memorial signpost, the highest point of the walk is reached and Anglezarke Moor comes into view, while looking back you can see Holcombe Tower. Now it's all downhill until, passing the ruins of Higher Pasture Barn, the outward route is re-joined back to the car park.

19

STEPPING ON JACOB'S LADDER

Lathkill Dale

LOCATION: 8 miles south east of Buxton

START: Lay-by on B5055 half a mile east of Monyash, toilets

DISTANCE: 3½ miles

GRADE: Moderate

TIME: 2 hours

BUS: From Buxton 177 & 350 (not Sun)

MAP: Outdoor Leisure - White Peak, Landranger 119

REFRESHMENTS: Monyash

From its upper narrow gorge, down past the deep cave where the river rises, to its vertical limestone cliffs, Lathkill Dale is a delight. In summer, the slopes are covered with harebells and thyme, hawkbit and rock roses, while the prize of the Nature Reserve is the purple-petalled Jacob's ladder. Climbing away from the valley, you come to the medieval One Ash Grange. The narrow fields beyond are a fossilised remnant of ancient strip farming patterns, and then there is Monyash. Once a major lead mining centre, its history goes back beyond Domesday and, amid the houses and pub clustered round the village green, the Market Cross has stood for 650 years.

THE ROUTE

From the lay-by on the B5055, a footpath sign points across a stile into Lathkill Dale. At first the dale is shallow and you walk through fields of buttercups, then the limestone cliffs close in to form a narrow gorge. A pile of tumbled boulders almost blocks the way and at their foot is an old mine level, driven in an unsuccessful attempt by Isaac Beresford in 1787 to drain the Magpie Mine on Sheldon Moor. Recently, cavers have linked the passage with Lathkill Head Cave: coincidentally, one of them was also called Beresford.

The boulders are spoil from Ricklow Quarry, where a decorative grey marble was mined until 1900. The blast holes can still be seen and the crinoidal fossils show up beautifully on the dark rocks, polished smooth by countless pairs of boots.

After a squeezer stile, the dry grassy dale opens out, bounded by steep slopes and high white cliffs, and here the rare Jacob's ladder can be found. The flower gets its name from the leaves, which are arranged like the rungs of a ladder, and there is more growing wild here than anywhere else in the country.

Although in wet weather the river appears from Lathkill Head Cave as a full-blown torrent, in summer the entrance to 2000ft of underground passages is often dry, tempting cavers to crawl flat-out into the darkness. But continuing down the valley, the river, one of the purest in the country, gradually appears. Reaching a footbridge, where stone walls hidden under vegetation are the remains of a medieval sheepwash, you turn right over the stream to wander up Cales Dale.

Ignoring the stepped path to the left, keep right, under a limestone cliff, to climb out of the dale. After crossing the field, a few steps up by a

Lathkill Dale

barn bring you to One Ash Grange, a 12th-century monastic sheep farm which belonged to Roche Abbey in Yorkshire.

Going past a Camping Barn, turn right and follow the track until, as the lane comes to an end, you turn right into a field and then immediately left beside the wall. Gradually climbing, there is little sign of the path until, in the corner, a rather slippery step stile leads into the next field. Now the spire of Monyash Church comes into view and the path continues over a series of stiles and past Fern Dale, an old lead rake. Then, becoming walled, the little lane wanders on past long, narrow fields, enclosed in the 16th century.

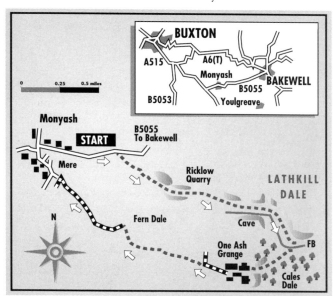

Reaching Monyash, turn right along Rakes Road past Fere Mere, the only survivor of the village's five original meres. Turning right again in front of the ancient Market Cross, you pass the Bull's Head, which dates from 1619, and continuing by St Leonard's Church, it is all downhill.

21

LIFE IN LYMM

Canal bridge at Lymm

LOCATION: 5 miles west of Altrincham
START: Just off A56, behind Lymm church.
Parking off Crouchley Lane
DISTANCE: 3½ miles
GRADE: Easy
TIME: 2 hours
BUS: From Altrincham: 37 & 38
MAP: Pathfinder 740, Landranger 109
REFRESHMENTS: Lymm

Everyone knows that squirrels love nuts, but the grey squirrels that live by Lymm Dam near Altrincham like bananas too. They are quite tame and as we ate our picnic they formed a circle round us, boldly darting in for a share. Leaving the lake, where moorhens, coots and mallards were busy, we continued beside the Duke of Bridgewater's Canal. Stately irises fringed the water and a solitary heron stood motionless, heedless of a passing barge. But on a hot sunny afternoon, we were glad of the shade along the bridlepath, where pink dog roses and red campion brightened the hedgerow.

THE ROUTE

Taking the footpath which runs beside the bridleway beneath magnificent horse-chestnut trees, fork right to walk by Lymm Dam. The lake was formed in the 1820s, when the new turnpike road to Manchester dammed the brook, and the park was originally landscaped by the first Lord Leverhulme, who planted the trees and improved the footpaths.

The path follows the lip of the steep slope above the lake shore with its ancient beeches, and through a picnic area where grey squirrels beg for food. Then reaching a sandy cliff you go over a couple of footbridges by a little waterfall, and turn right along the far side of the lake towards the arched dam.

Crossing the A56, the footpath continues down through the tall trees of The Dingle, where the bright blue bellflower grows beside Bradley Brook. The roots of this plant were once used as a treatment for sore throats. Emerging into the centre of Lymm by Lower Dam, Bridgewater Street lies to the left and this leads up to join the canal, where brightly painted narrow boats crowd the water's edge. The Bridgewater was the first canal to be built in England, and the section that joined Worsley to Runcorn via Lymm was constructed around 1770.

Turning right past the Golden Fleece, you can see the ancient sandstone Market Cross in the square below, where John Wesley once preached. The road bridge is then crossed, and you turn right again and continue beside the canal past the moored barges of Lymm Cruising Club.

Soon the tall spire of Oughtrington Church comes into view across the fields, while beside the towpath red and white clover, common cat's-ear and meadow buttercups are a mass of colour in summer.

At the next bridge, where tow ropes have bitten deep into the brickwork, cross to the other side of the canal and double back along the bridleway. This pleasant shady path leads between ancient hawthorn hedges past fields, then veering away from the canal the road is reached by a primary school.

In about 100 yards, turn left up Orchard Avenue, and at the end of the road turn right, taking the upper path which follows the edge of a grassy field behind some houses. Joining the road,

Cottage by Bradley Brook, Lymm

continue in the same direction to the main road. On the far side, a path leads to the right of St Mary's Church, the fourth to be built on this site, and down to Lymm Dam. Passing a sculpted sandstone outcrop, a stepped path then climbs behind the church back to the start of the walk.

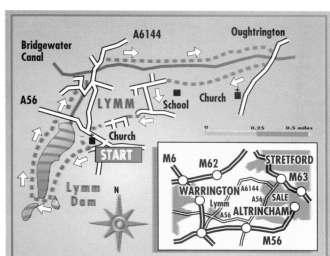

23

ON THE POINT OF PARADISE

LOCATION: 7 miles south of Southport

START: Lifeboat Road Car Park, Formby

DISTANCE: 3½ (or 2) miles

GRADE: Easy

TIME: 2 hours

TRAIN: Formby

MAP: Pathfinder 710, Landranger 108

REFRESHMENTS: Formby

Tide coming in, Formby

From its golden, gently shelving beach to its massive, wind-sculpted sand dunes, Formby Point, near Southport, is a paradise for children. Red squirrels scamper up the tall pines, meadow pipits, yellowhammers and whitethroats nest among the scrub, while sand lizards and the rare natterjack toad make their home on the grasslands. Summer sees cinnabar and burnet moths and many brightly coloured butterflies. And then there are the flowers - golden trumpets of the evening primrose, dog roses, drifts of pink thrift and yellow mats of the biting stonecrop. So don't forget to bring your flower book and a pair of binoculars, as well as a bucket and spade.

THE ROUTE

Walk back towards Lifeboat Road, but just before reaching the tarmac, turn left on a sandy path through an open area. Staying parallel to the road, the path enters scrubby woodland then, crossing a footpath and a permissive bridlepath, continues uphill into the pinewoods. These were planted in the 1920s to stabilize the dunes and red squirrels may often be seen here.

Now the route turns left through the pines until, after crossing a sandy track, you bear left along the edge of the wood through a picnic area. Reaching Wick's Lane Lake, turn left along the board walk, where tall yellow spikes of evening primrose bloom beside pools made in 1978, while almost hidden in the grass is the tiny pink-flowered centaury.

The path leads past open grasslands where faint traces remain of old furrowed asparagus fields, then passing a belt of trees, and crossing the Sefton coastal footpath, continues beside Wicks Wood. The sea is still out of sight beyond the massive dunes, and veering left the path joins the route to the beach. The board walk has recently been replaced, for it was swept away by storms.

From the shore, an oil drilling platform can be seen, while to the north lies Blackpool Tower with a backdrop of the Lake District mountains. On our visit, the shipping channel was busy with cargo boats and the Isle of Man ferry, but most exciting of all was the unexpected arrival of the QE2, on its way to dock at Liverpool.

Dune Landsape

Turning left, walk along the windswept beach beside the sand dunes. Constantly being eroded, they are protected by chestnut pailings and last year's Christmas Trees, planted by local school children to trap the sand. Passing the Car Park North Marker, the Short Route turns back along a good path at the Car Park South Marker.

The longer route continues along the beach past the site of the first lifeboat station in Britain, built in 1776, though the ruins are of a later station built in 1809. Passing the Nature Reserve Marker, the route turns inland at the Alexandra Road Marker. The Rifle Range, which lies further along the beach, is barred to walkers when the red flags are flying.

White posts mark the route through the high dune ridge, then slithering down the sandy slope you join a broad, unsurfaced track which heads away from the beach. Passing a red brick mansion, turn left, then in a few yards, at the edge of Shorrocks Hill woodland, you go left again into Ravenmeols Nature Reserve.

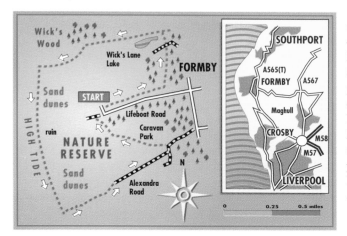

Follow the picket fence, then at the corner a narrow path keeps straight on. Skirting the caravan park, little paths invite exploration of the Nature Reserve, before heading for the end of the row of pine trees, you are back at Lifeboat Road and the car park.

WIN ALL THE WAY

LOCATION: Hope, 8 miles east of
Chapel-en-le-Frith
START: Hope car park on A625, toilets
DISTANCE: 5½ miles
GRADE: Strenuous
TIME: 3 hours
TRAIN: Hope
MAP: Outdoor Leisure - Dark Peak,
Landranger 110
REFRESHMENTS: Hope

Ladybower Reservoir from Win Hill

Despite its name, peaks are rather rare in the Peak District, but Win Hill, above the village of Hope, has all the essential qualities. Reaching 1,516ft, the hill supposedly gets its name from being the camp of the victorious King Edwin of Northumbria when he fought the King of Wessex, though more likely 'Win' refers to bilberries. But any mountain would be proud to have this summit, a steep-sided gritstone outcrop crowned with a trig point. And in August, the hill is at its very best, for the slopes are covered in purple heather and as you walk high above the valley, the air is filled with clouds of pollen, the scent of honey and the hum of bees.

THE ROUTE

From the car park, turn right, then opposite St Peter's Church, go left up Edale Road. Above the houses, the distinctive summit of Win Hill can be seen, then in 400 yards the pavement comes to an end and you fork right to cross the River Noe at Killhill Bridge.

The road goes beneath the railway, which links Manchester to Sheffield, and turning left begins to climb gently. Then, at the entrance to The Homestead, you fork left on a track to the Coach House where a squeezer stile brings you into the field.

Passing Fullwood Stile Farm, a tree-shaded lane is joined which leads steadily uphill. This is the Roman Road which led to Glossop from the fort of Navio in the valley below. Field roses bloom in the hedge and to the left Lose Hill can be seen. At a gate, the open moor is gained, and leaving the track a path begins to climb more steeply. Now the Vale of Edale is in view, and beyond the patchwork fields rises the escarpment shape of Crookstone Knoll, the end of the Kinder plateau.

Above us, a kestrel hovered, hanging on the wind, while below a tractor toiled to and fro, turning the hay in long parallel lines. Bracken, a very invasive weed, covers the flanks of the hill, but as height is gained rough grass takes over. The heathery top is the crowning glory of Win Hill, and as the angle eases you turn right to follow the wide path along the broad ridge. Sheep lay panting in the shade of the walls, while above us half a dozen paragliders, with their multi-coloured canopies, floated in the up-currents.

Win Hill summit

Win Hill is one of the best summits in the Peak, and from the trig point on the rocky top there is an extensive view all around. On the eastern horizon is the high gritstone escarpment of Stanage Edge; to the west lies Kinder; while northwards Bleaklow stretches into the blue distance.

The descent is at first back the way you came, but as the path flattens out, you fork left across the heather. A stony path slants down across the hillside to a stile and then a couple of very steep grassy fields bring you to Twitchill Farm. Follow the farm track down until, meeting your outward route, you go under the railway and along to the River Noe.

Just before the bridge, take the track on the left to Hope Corn Mill, whose date of 1886 refers to its restoration, because the site is much older. Immediately after the house, go left over a stile into the field. A path then leads beside the river to emerge onto the A625, where you turn right back into Hope.

Anne on Win Hill summit

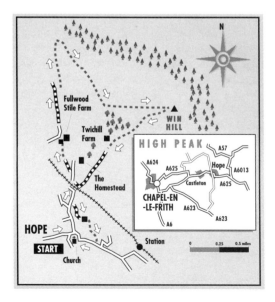

27

GOING WITH THE GRANE

View from Stony Rake

LOCATION: 2 miles west of Haslingden

START: Clough Head Quarry car park on the B6232, toilets

DISTANCE: 3 miles

GRADE: Easy, but with some ascent.

TIME: 2 hours

NOTE: Information Centre open summer weekend afternoons

BUS: From Blackburn: 236

MAP: Explorer - West Pennine Moors, Landranger 103

REFRESHMENTS: Pack a flask

In the low slanting rays of the afternoon sun, with the blue sheen of open water appearing through the branches of larch and beech, Haslingden Grane is enchanting. Once a hunting ground for the ancient Forest of Rossendale, the woods were cleared for farmers and weavers, but in 1912 Ogden Reservoir was built and the valley abandoned. Above the chain of three lakes, old deserted farmsteads, the home of the 'Whisky Spinners' who concealed their stills in secret passages, stand starkly on the hillside. But beside the becks the trees are coming back, a home to meadow pipits, tree-creepers and even the tiny goldcrest, Britain's smallest bird.

THE ROUTE

To the left of the Information Centre, a concession path goes over a stile, then climbs beside the wall to join an old rush-filled track along the hillside. There is a bird's-eye view of the car park, once the site of a brickworks, while across the valley is the old quarry on Musbury Heights, which closed in the 1920s. Turning left, follow the wall past the wood, then cross a stile and descend to the busy Grane Road.

Go left for a few yards and take the second footpath, known as Stony Rake. This old packhorse way was the main route through the valley until 1810, when it was replaced by the turnpiked Grane Road. There are splendid views across the head of the Grane Valley where farms, abandoned when the reservoir was built, follow the line of emergent springs on the hillside.

Passing an old slate pit, which pre-dates the more modern quarries, the track becomes enclosed and you turn downhill between stone walls. The path continues over a stile and through the trees to join another track, which leads down to the grand ruins of Lower Ormerods. Built of Haslingden flagstone, the house belonged to one of the richest local families.

Crossing the bridge beside Calf Hey Reservoir, you climb again, up the steps and past pine trees planted in the 1960s. There are long views down the lake to Haslingden and its surrounding high moors, while beside the path, two stone gate-posts and a ruin are all that remains of Grane Head, once used as a school and chapel. A footbridge leads over a clough once known as 'Th' Hell Hoile', but renamed by the local clergyman, in true tasteful Victorian fashion, as the Fairy Glen.

Passing a fine beech wood and a larch plantation, you cross Hog Lowe Clough, and turn up the stream before continuing along the hillside. A couple of stiles lead out of the wood and the little trod bumbles along the open moor. Beside the path grows the bright yellow-green lemon-scented fern, easily identified by its smell when the fronds are crushed.

At a large sycamore tree, a path leads downhill to cross the castellated dam. This collapsed during its construction in 1856 and had to be rebuilt. A tarmac footpath then leads uphill and through a small car park on the site of Chapel Row whose terrace of 18th century cottages is long gone, and only the chapel graveyard remains.

Ogden Resevoir

A footpath turns off left to Clough Head, climbing through newly planted broad-leaved trees to reach Grane Road. Turn left and cross to the gate back into the old quarry, but take care, it is a busy road and we value our readers!

Fairy Glen

CHESHIRE'S MATTERHORN

Steps on the ascent

LOCATION: 5 miles south east of Macclesfield

START: Wildboarclough, Vicarage Quarry car park (GR 984706)

DISTANCE: 4 miles

GRADE: Strenuous

TIME: 2 hours

MAP: Outdoor Leisure - White Peak, Landranger 118

REFRESHMENTS: Crag Inn

Rising like an Alpine peak above the dark conifers of Macclesfield Forest, Shutlingsloe is Cheshire's Matterhorn. Its instantly recognisable profile is one to catch the imagination, and the view from the top is magnificent, extending far over the Peak District, and across the Cheshire Plain to the Welsh mountains and the South Pennine hills. Beneath its steep slopes, the lovely valley of Wildboarclough was reputedly named in 1610 after the last wild boar in England was killed here. But though the name more likely comes from the Old English 'boore', meaning a hillside, the village stands on the fringe of a medieval hunting forest, so maybe there is some truth in the story after all.

THE ROUTE

Turning left out of the old quarry to follow the quiet road up the valley beside Clough Brook, it is hard to believe that on 24 May 1989, this stream swelled to a roaring torrent. Bridges were washed away and widespread devastation was caused in Wildboarclough, but now the only signs of the disaster are the newly rebuilt walls. Leaving the road just past Dingers Hollow Farm, a footpath slants across the fields, heading towards a barn. A lane is joined at a stile by a gate then, after climbing to the memorial stone at the crest of the hill, you turn left on the concession bridleway.

Follow the track along the edge of the wood into the dense trees of Macclesfield Forest, which dates back to medieval times. Dipping to pass Ferriser, built in 1828 but abandoned a century later when Trentabank Reservoir was constructed, the track then climbs gently to a clearing at the top of the hill where, a few yards to the left, a stile leads onto the open moor.

It is now a steady plod up the flagged path, created in 1992 with the aid of a helicopter to replace a muddy and eroded route. Soon the shapely cone of Shutlingsloe comes into view, then, crossing a boardwalk to a stile, you turn right along the gritstone wall. Reaching another stile, the angle steepens, and steps climb the last few feet to the rocky peak.

Shutlingsloe, descent to Wildboarclough

The white painted concrete trig point feels much higher than its 1659ft, and a topograph details the surrounding hills. Though the summit rocks of Scyttel's Hill, as it was once called, are decorated with 19th century graffiti, the right of way over the top was not official until 1980.

Way-marks point straight down the steep slope, but the path finds an easy way through the rocks and on down the hillside to a stile. This is the route of the annual fell race from Crag Hall, in the valley below, which takes place each Spring Bank Holiday Monday. The record to the top and back is an amazing 15 minutes 35 seconds.

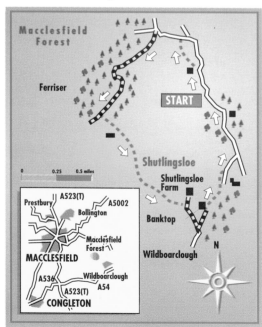

Crossing the rough pasture, another stile is reached near Shutlingsloe Farm, then the path follows a wall to the tarmac farm road, where you turn right. Reaching a cattle grid by a gate, a path doubles back to pass Banktop, an attractive 17th century cottage, and continues by a sturdy gritstone barn and above a larch plantation. Crossing a little stream, you join the valley road, and turning left, past Clough House car park, which was swept away by the floods, it is now just half a mile of road walking back to Vicarage Quarry.

THE NIGHT THE DAM BURST

Marsden Clough

LOCATION: 3 miles south west of Holmfirth

START: Digley Reservoir North Car Park

DISTANCE: 5½ miles

GRADE: Moderate

TIME: 3 hours

BUS: From Manchester: 180 Sat, 429 Suns & Bank Holidays

MAP: Outdoor Leisure - Dark Peak, Landranger 110

REFRESHMENTS: Holme

On the northern fringe of the Dark Peak, where the Pennine Way descends from the wilderness of Black Hill, is a spur of heather moorland. Incised by the steep-sided Marsden Clough, the area is quiet and deserted, and sees few people, yet straight-line walls still divide the landscape, and looping across the hillside is a clear and obvious track. Once this was a cart road serving a thriving local community. But with the coming of the reservoirs, the farms were abandoned, leaving a legacy of ancient pathways, while the moor is the preserve of the curlew, skylark, and the grouse.

THE ROUTE

From the entrance to the car park, sited in the quarry that provided the stone for Digley Dam, take the walled track leading gently uphill. As the track levels out, go right, over a stone stepstile, to follow a narrow path through the heather, past an old quarry. Climbing steeply to a wooden stepstile, the path enters a field and continues up to a ruined farm, where you turn left. Already you feel high above the valley, while on the skyline is the winking Holme Moss mast on Black Hill.

The broad old road leads up the valley and, ignoring side turnings, you pass the buildings at Greaves Head, abandoned in the 1840s when Bilberry Reservoir was constructed. Just 12 years later, there was one of the worst reservoir disasters in the country when the dam burst in the middle of the night, killing 81 people in the valley below.

Nether Lane winds its way on through the fields past Bartin, once the head gamekeeper's house, and climbs to the shooting box of Goodbent Lodge. Keep a look out for speeding mountain bikers as this is a tempting downhill slope. Before you reach the sharp bend ahead, turn left over a gritstone stepstile and take the footpath to Wessenden Head Moor, now owned by brewers Bass.

A tumbled wall leads downhill, while on the skyline, to the right of the television mast, a cairn marks the line of the Pennine Way. In Marsden Clough at the meeting of two streams, a dilapidated footbridge stands beside gritstone abutments These are the remains of Blackpool Bridge, swept away by a cloudburst in 1944 when three people were drowned.

Climbing again the shooter's track leads uphill onto the moor where, among the heather and bilberry, the feathery tufts of cotton grass dance in the breeze. An old gatepost serves as a bridge in Hey Clough, then veering away from the stream the path joins Issues Road. The name refers to the allocation of land, when the fields were enclosed in the early 19th century, and several farms once stood here.

The long, straight lane leads gently downhill towards the Holme Valley. Keeping straight on at the junction, and past a convenient seat at a viewpoint, the lane curves round to the right. Just before a house, you turn sharp left, down a gated track and continue down the clough to Digley Reservoir.

Turn left and, after a little gated stile, the path crosses the broad stone dam of Bilberry Reservoir and zigzags up the hill.

Digley Reservoir

Keep straight on past impressive stone gateposts, all that remains of a former mill owner's mansion, and the track joins a flight of steps which leads back to the quarry and the car park.

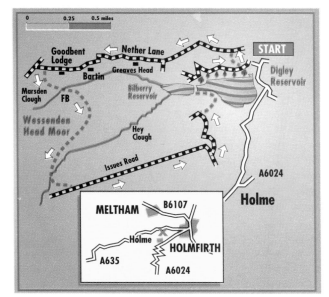

Greaves Head barns

33

BEACON OF SOLITUDE

Summit of Beacon Fell

LOCATION: 8 miles north of Preston

START: Beacon Fell, Fell House car park.
Signed from Broughton on A6, toilets

DISTANCE: 5 miles

TIME: 2½ hours

GRADE: Moderate

NOTE: Visitor Centre Tel: 01995 640557

BUS: From Preston Z4 (not Sun)

MAP: Outdoor Leisure - Forest of Bowland,
Landranger 102

REFRESHMENTS: Visitor Centre

Standing a little apart in the Forest of Bowland, the isolated shape of Beacon Fell rises above the valley of the River Brock. Fields and a maze of country lanes lead down to the river where dense woodland cloaks the banks and you make your way along quiet footpaths beside the rippling water. Then, emerging from the trees, the skyline is full of the wild Bowland Fells and, with a great feeling of space and solitude, you climb across rough pastures, until reaching the summit of Beacon Fell you look out on a panorama that reaches to the Lake District.

THE ROUTE

Above the Visitor Centre, a path leads left along the hillside through the trees, then forking left you come down to the road. Cross straight over to a stile into the fields where there is an extensive view over The Fylde to Morecambe Bay. Continue downhill to a little footbridge and follow the fence to the road.

Turning right and then left, the tree-shaded White Lee Lane leads gently down to Higher Brock Bridge. Go through the stone gateposts, and fork left in front of Brock Mill, a former corn mill. The track goes into the field and you follow the fence on the right to the river, where fragrant meadow sweet and purple knapweed cover the banks beneath the crumbling shaley cliffs.

The narrow path enters a wood, then climbs away from the river to join a track where you turn left. Reaching Paradise Cottage, inscribed WW1721, leave the track to follow the edge of a wood. Just when you are beginning to have doubts about the route, a section of boardwalk is reached, and the path continues by the river to a footbridge.

Turn right up Snape Rake Lane, which soon becomes tarmac, then at the end of the wood you go left along an old track barred by a field gate. At the hairpin bend, a slithery path goes steeply down into a little clough and, climbing the far bank, you continue along the field edge. A track is then joined which leads through the Scout camp to a stile into the fields.

Head across to a gate, then stay by the river to reach a wooden footbridge. Don't cross, but turn right to a stile where steps and boardwalks lead to another footbridge. Climbing out of the clough, you emerge from the trees with a view ahead of the long ridge of Fair Snape Fell.

Keep straight on, then turn right beside the fence to the yard of Wickins Barn, which dates from 1850. Turning right, the honeysuckle fringed lane leads round a bend and you take the track to Broadhead Farm. The route goes through the gateway of Heatherway Farm, once prosaically known as 'Weedacre',

Farm on the slopes of Beacon fell

then reaching the house, the footpath has been diverted and you go right over a stile before turning left in a few yards to climb to the road.

A path opposite slants up through the conifers of Beacon Fell then, turning left briefly on the broad path, take the little trod which leads up over rough grass to the trig point. From this ancient beacon site Black Combe, on the fringe of the Lake District, looks remarkably close and the summit feels much higher than its 873ft.

Keep straight on, then follow the paved way which bends right, down to Sheepfold Picnic Area, where turning right brings you back to the Visitor Centre.

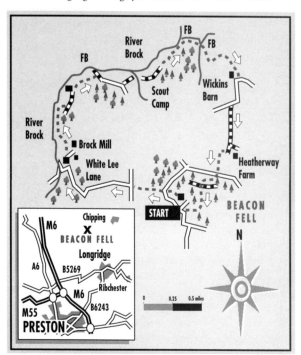

Bridge, River Brock

JAGGERS AND STONES

LOCATION: 14 miles east of Glossop

START: Cutthroat Bridge on the A57, lay-by 200 yards up the road

DISTANCE: 5 (or 4) miles

GRADE: Moderate

TIME: 3 hours

BUS: 373(Summer Sun & BH Mon). From Rochdale via Glossop 473

MAP: Outdoor Leisure - Dark Peak, Landranger 110

REFRESHMENTS: Ladybower Inn

Wheel Stones

On the eastern rim of the Peak District, high above Ladybower Reservoir, the distinctive shape of the Wheel Stones stands against the sky. This gritstone tor, carved by wind and weather, is more popularly called the Coach and Horses, for its outline looks remarkably like a stage coach with a team of four. Once Jaggers passed this way, leading their long lines of pack ponies, and a guidestone still marks the route. Then, as you follow the ancient tracks across the moor, shooting butts stand in line like sentries and the grouse spring up from beneath your feet with their startled cry "Go back. Go back!".

THE ROUTE

From the lay-by, walk down the main road to Cutthroat Bridge, which got its name from a murder in 1635, and turn right through the gate. In a few yards, as the track rounds a corner, leave it to cross Highshaw Clough and follow a grassy footpath under the power lines. At first flanked by bracken, the old packhorse way leads on across a grassy moor speckled with the yellow four-petalled tormentil, then just beyond the stepstile there is an old guidestone. Erected in 1737 by Act of Parliament, this stood on 'the common way' which led from Sheffield to Hope.

Reaching a gate, with Moscar House straight ahead, turn left to follow the old Jagger's Route, signed to Derwent. The track leads uphill and at a gate the open moor is reached. After crossing Highshaw Clough, the path forks, and taking the lower branch, marked with a rickety signpost, you pass several substantial shooting butts, for this is an active grouse moor.

Gradually climbing, the bracken gives way to heather, until after a mile the path reaches Derwent Edge and suddenly the view opens out. Far below is Ladybower Reservoir, across the valley stands Win Hill with Kinder beyond, while to the north in the blue distance is Bleaklow.

A visit to Wheel Stones is an out and back, and turning right along the clear sandy path, soon the weathered tor comes in sight, with the ridge beyond stretching to the trig point on Back Tor.

Returning now to the junction, keep straight on, following the escarpment edge. The path avoids Hurkling Stones to make straight for Whinstone Lee Tor, which is a good viewpoint poised on the edge with Ladybower Reservoir far below. The reservoir, which drowned the

High on Derwent Edge

village of Ashopton, was begun in 1935 and completed eight years later, but on our last visit mud flats were exposed and it held only a small fraction of its full complement of 6300 million gallons.

When you reach a six-way junction, the old packhorse route to the left is a short cut back to Cutthroat Bridge, but turning the opposite way follow the gully heading directly for the reservoir. Curving left, the path keeps by the wall down to a plantation fringed with oak and silver birch.

Emerging from the trees at a gate, the houses below stand on the fringe of the old village of Ashopton. Continue along the track, through the upper gate, across the hillside with the reservoir in view below and Bamford Edge on the skyline. After entering the trees, a track comes up from the right and it is only a few yards detour down to the Ladybower Inn. The track then climbs a little up onto the moor and a wide path continues beneath the power lines back to Cutthroat Bridge.

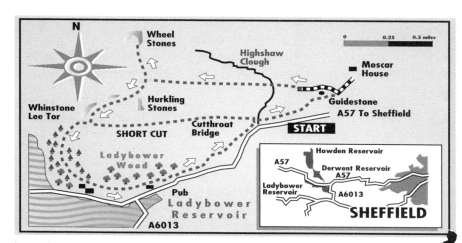

STOP AND GORPLE

LOCATION: 3 miles east of Burnley (Grid reference 882313)

START: Hurstwood car park

DISTANCE: 5½ miles

GRADE: Moderate

TIME: 3 hours

BUS: From Burnley to Worsthorne 1, 2, 4 & 7

NOTE: Navigation tricky in mist, take a compass

MAP: Outdoor Leisure - South Pennines, Landranger 103

REFRESHMENTS: Pack a flask

Hurstwood Hall

It was late afternoon. To the west, the sun was sinking into a thin veil of cloud, and Burnley had long vanished into a smoky haze, but up on the Lancashire-Yorkshire border we had the moor to ourselves. The silvery heads of wavy hair-grass rippled in the breeze, below us gleamed the blue sheen of a reservoir and on the skyline was the gaunt outline of Gorple Stones. Though the village of Hurstwood, with its delightful cluster of Elizabethan houses, is hardly more than a stone's throw from Burnley, as you climb towards Worsthorne Moor you enter a different world where meadow pipits fly suddenly from beneath your feet and the only sound is of the streams.

THE ROUTE

From the car park, go back towards Hurstwood Hall, which was built by Barnard Towneley in 1579, and turn right past the telephone box. As the road comes to an end, you cross a stile, and a way-mark of the Burnley Way points you up the hill to the top of the wood. The climb continues beside the pine plantation, with its fringe of beech, and briefly the view opens out. Hurstwood Reservoir gleams through the trees, but soon the westward view is hemmed in by a waterboard gritstone wall.

As the plantation comes to an end, ahead is Worsthorne Moor and a vast expanse of grass-covered mounds like the moraines of an ancient glacier. Yet though these are only spoil heaps, this landscape owes much to the Ice Age for the miners were seeking limestone boulders transported here by glaciers. The workings date back to the 17th century when streams were dammed and then suddenly released to strip away the surface soil.

Descending to the path below, which brings you to a footbridge, follow the stream, then fork left, recrossing the brook. The path leads up a little valley into North West Water's Access Land and on to Gorple Road. It is a steady climb on this ancient track and, while an occasional patch of cross-leaved heath is a splash of colour among the crowberry and bilberry, mainly the moor is rough grass.

Gorple Upper Reservoir from Gorple Stones

After Hurstwood Brook is crossed, the angle eases, then approaching Rams Clough a concession path heads downhill, which shortens the route by half a mile, but the track climbs on to a notice at Spring Head. Gorple Stones, a collection of silver-grey gritstone rocks, is high on the moor to the left, and ahead Gorple Upper Reservoir lies in a bowl beneath the hills.

Hare Stones, down to the right, is the next objective. Turn off just beyond the wooden sign and a clear path appears in a few yards which follows the grassy ridge. Reaching the gritstone outcrop, continue to the lowest point on the col where a faint groove to the right marks the start of a narrow trod leading down to Rams Clough.

After crossing the stream, the path climbs to join the much clearer concession path where you go left, but in a few yards take the right fork to follow the less obvious path heading for the bumpy ridge. These are the tips of an old quarry - beware of steep drops - and then a wide grassy track is joined which contours the hillside above Cant Clough Reservoir.

Joining the gravelled track coming up from the dam, this leads down to Hurstwood Reservoir where you turn left across the leat and down the tarmac road back to the car park.

39

A TRAIL OF THREE CASTLES

Elephant and Castle

LOCATION: 12 miles south west of Northwich

START: Beeston Castle (Sandstone Trail car park, not the one opposite the castle), toilets

DISTANCE: 5 miles

GRADE: Moderate

TIME: 2½ hours

NOTE: Beeston Castle open daily (tel: 01829 260464)

BUS: From Chester: C83 (Mon-Sat)

MAP: Pathfinder 790, Landranger 117

REFRESHMENTS: Pack a flask

Far out on the Cheshire Plain, rising above its encircling cloak of trees, the distinctive outline of Beeston Castle has stood as a landmark for over 700 years. Yet though castles are a rarity in Cheshire, here is an abundance, for only a longbow shot away on the opposite hill is another. But Peckforton Castle is a newcomer, planned for style rather than defence. Just 150 years old, these sandstone ramparts were built by Admiral Sir John Tollemache, while the commanding view of the Mersey was chosen so that his wife could watch for his ship coming home.

THE ROUTE

From the car park, turn left and follow the Sandstone Trail beside the high stone wall, then fork left along the edge of the plantation down to the road. Crossing over to the left of Tabernacle Cottage, a footpath leads through the field to a little footbridge and continues out to a lane where you turn right.

Beeston Castle, built as part of the Welsh border defences, looks down on the fields, then passing the half-timbered Moat House you go left into the Peckforton Estate. The sandy track climbs gently through the oak wood, while between the trees there are glimpses of the Cheshire Plain stretching westwards to the River Dee.

At the crossroads, the Sandstone Trail keeps straight on until, at a signpost by a bend, you strike off left. It is then only a short climb to the top of the sandstone ridge. Don't go over the stile, but turn right and in 100 yards the edge of the wood is reached. Continuing across the fields, the view now extends to the far Welsh hills.

Reaching the road, go left, then left again at the T-junction by the white cottage. The Sandstone Trail now turns away, but continuing down Hill Lane into the wood you come to a bridge. This took carriages to Peckforton Castle and is said to be haunted by a headless figure. Just after the arch, go right and over a stile into the fields. Now the view is eastwards, and beyond the interlocking jigsaw of fields are the distant blue hills of the Peak District.

Beeston Castle above the trees

Heading for the farm with the black and white gable, way-marked stiles point the way down to an ancient oak, where John Wesley once preached, then going through a small Christmas tree plantation, the road is reached at a half-timbered thatched cottage. Go left through the hamlet of Peckforton and past Laundry Cottage with its striking sculpture of the Elephant and Castle. Carved from solid stone by the mason who built the real castle at Peckforton, this was intended as a beehive.

Continuing along the road you pass several attractive houses, but in the heyday of the Peckforton Estate there were many more. The millstone in the wall opposite Keepers Cottage came from the local mill. Just before the grand lodge of Peckforton Castle, a stile, signed Beeston Moss, leads into the fields. With both castles now in view, head for a pair of trees and continue over the rising ground to a stile at the centre of Willis's Wood.

Emerging from the trees, aim to the right of the farm buildings where a stile leads onto a muddy track and just beyond is the road. Turn left then after passing Brook Farm, fork right and in a few yards a sign points you back to Beeston Castle.

41

TWIN-EDGED PARADE

LOCATION: Rowarth, 4 miles east of Marple

START: Rowarth Village car park (Grid reference 012893)

DISTANCE: 4 miles

GRADE: Moderate

TIME: 2 hours

MAP: Outdoor Leisure - Dark Peak, Landranger 110

REFRESHMENTS: Little Mill Inn, Rowarth

On Combes Edge

Looking up at Coombes Edge, poised on the skyline near Glossop, it seems as though a giant has taken a huge bite out of the hillside. And he left a few teeth behind as well, for high on the edge the rocks stick up like fangs. Yet though an approach from the west presents an obvious challenge, we decided to avoid the full frontal assault and instead sneak up round the back from Rowarth, one of the most secret hamlets in the Peak District. This route also reveals the hidden side of the hill, for here is Cown Edge, and two edges in one walk is good value indeed!

THE ROUTE

From the car park, follow the road into Rowarth, then keep straight on past Poplar Farm and take the footpath on the left signed Cown Edge. Though now a peaceful scene, this village once had three cotton mills. Hemmed in by fences, it is a steady climb and at a double stile the moor is reached.

Continuing up beside the gritstone wall by a disused quarry, you come to a five-way signpost, and following the finger which points to Cown Edge, the climb continues. Already Rowarth is a long way below, while the eastern view expands to take in Lantern Pike and the more distant slopes of the Kinder plateau. Grassed-over mounds are all that remain of old coal pits, then reaching a stile on the skyline the angle eases and the route forks right across the moor.

Climbing the stile into the next field, head across to the far corner where a hidden stile is revealed, and beyond is a track. Turn left along this to a small gate, then a path on the right leads to Coombes Edge. The arrival is sudden and from this dramatic crest you look down on the green fields of the Etherow Valley and across Stockport to the far blue distance. This huge scoop in the hillside was created by a landslip during the Ice Age.

It is an easy stroll along the rim, but take care as there are steep drops. Passing a narrow fringe of woodland, the pines stunted by exposure to the wind, continue for about 200 yards to a stile. A grassy track between wire fences then leads across the moor to the east-facing gritstone quarries of Cown Edge.

The old post office, Rowarth

The path swings right and downhill to Rocks Farm, where you go left to follow the track out past Higher Plainstead Farm to the Monk's Road. This was used by monks from Basingwerk Abbey in Flint, who owned land here in the 12th century, and runs closely parallel with the Roman Road that linked Glossop with Buxton.

At the road junction, a footpath sign points right, and you head down to the bottom corner of the field to join a lane. Keep straight on and the tarmac is followed until, at the bend, a squeezer stile leads onto Matley Moor. A path through the heather then brings you to a track where you go right and out to rejoin the lane. Carry on downhill past Kings Clough Head Farm, and at the road end a track continues down to a ford.

Balancing over on the stepping stones, turn left and follow the path along the valley beside the stream. Continuing through woodland, a track is crossed at a stile, and the path brings you into Rowarth by the Old Post Office, where you turn right back to the car park.

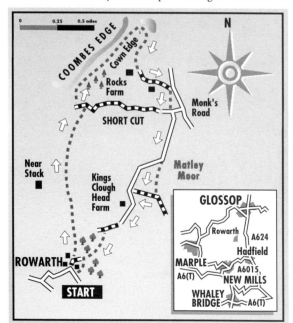

FOR LIMERS, NOT CLIMBERS

The Dobbin Stone

LOCATION: Between Bacup and Todmorden

START: Lay-by at summit of A681

DISTANCE: 4½ (or 2½) miles

GRADE: Moderate

TIME: 2½ hours

NOTE: The walk crosses rough, boggy moorland, boots essential

BUS: Todmorden to Rawtenstall: 33 Mon-Sat; 50 Sun only

MAP: Outdoor Leisure - South Pennines, Landranger 103

REFRESHMENTS: Pack a flask

A walk on the high moors without any climbing sounds impossible, but here, on the ridge that divides Bacup from Todmorden, the walking is on the level. The secret, of course, is that you start at the top, right up on the Pennine Watershed itself, where two long distance paths follow the county boundary. One is modern, a 45 mile circular walk over the skyline of Rossendale. But Limers Gate dates back to the 17th century, when Galloway ponies carried lime from Craven and Bowland to sweeten the acidic Pennine land. And is there really no ascent? Well, perhaps a little, and it's a bit rough, but for a small effort the reward is great.

THE ROUTE

Walk down the main road towards Todmorden for about 200 yards, then take the track on the right, signed Limers Gate. Forking left, this ancient route from Rochdale to Clitheroe leads along the hillside. Traces remain of old coalmine workings, while below in the valley the Amateur Astronomy Centre can be seen. This was built on the site of the former 'Middle Shop' pipeworks, whose broken pipes have been used to repair the track.

Climbing gently and rounding the bend, the old road stretches on across the hillside towards more abandoned mines. After the wall turns away to the left, a sign points off the track and you fork right to follow Limers Gate, a grassy path waymarked with blue-topped stakes. Down in the valley, Gorpley Reservoir comes into view, while up on the moor a line of posts and stones marks the boundary between Lancashire and Yorkshire. The path then bends right towards a ladder stile where the Rossendale Way is joined. Here the Short Route turns back beside the wall.

Don't cross the stile, but turn left and follow the wall along the ridge until a signpost is reached at the wall bend. An old boundary stone which lies nearby is known as the Dobbin Stone. The route now goes through a gate into a field and continues in the same direction to the broken wall ahead. There is an extensive view over Rossendale and the Whitworth Valley to the isolated bump of Cowpe Low, while ahead the ridge stretches on over the rounded tops of Hades Hill and Brown Wardle Hill.

Follow the wall for a short way, then turn left, aiming for a wooden stile in the far corner. Another stile leads over the wall, which is then followed to the whitewashed trig point on Trough Edge End. There is a splendid view over Calderdale: Todmorden lies in the valley below and on the skyline Stoodley Pike stands prominent.

To return, retrace your steps to the ladder stile, then continue along the wall, still following the Rossendale Way, though there is little sign of a path over the grassy moor. To the left is the rounded hump of Hogshead Law Hill, then passing another toppled boundary stone you cross the flat, soggy Reaps Moss and beyond rises Tooter Hill, which means 'lookout'.

Finally, the Rossendale Way joins a farm track and it is now only a short distance back to the main road. But we have yet to solve the mystery of the moor. What are the strange concrete cylinders in the fence? Does anyone know?

What is it?

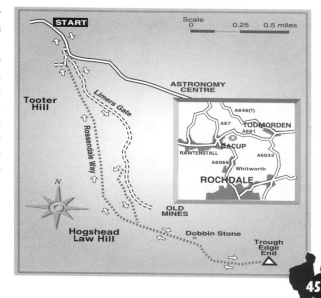

THE RICHES OF CHESHIRE

Pool near Woodend Farm

LOCATION: 4 miles south of Wilmslow

START: Prestbury Village Car Park, off Shirleys Drive

DISTANCE: 5½ miles

GRADE: Easy

TIME: 3 hours

BUS: From Macclesfield 19 (not Sun)

TRAIN: Prestbury

MAP: Pathfinder 759, Landranger 118

REFRESHMENTS: Prestbury

Set amid some of the loveliest Cheshire countryside, the picture-book village of Prestbury has a prosperous air. Neat whitewashed cottages, shops and restaurants are surrounded by immaculate farms and grand mansions. The name means Priests' Town, and this was a major monastic settlement in the Middle Ages. But Prestbury has always been an exclusive sort of place - it was ex-directory even in 1086 when it was omitted from the Domesday Book - and these days is regarded as possibly Britain's wealthiest village.

THE ROUTE

A signed footpath leads from the car park into Prestbury village, where you turn right past the shops and the church, then reaching Bollin Grove, with its row of 18th century cottages, you go left beside the river.

Keep straight on and the road becomes a track which continues across the river to Spittle House, whose name recalls its use as a hospital in the 17th century. The way-marked path goes left beside the garden hedge and continues through the fields to a willow-shrouded stream. Follow the field edge up, and turn left to pass a pond where trees have been planted by the Bollin Valley Project, which manages over 100 miles of footpaths.

Joining a track by a large, new barn, this leads out to the drive of Woodend Farm. Cross straight over, and way-marks point the way across the field to a couple of signposts and a stile in the field corner. Passing another new plantation, and ignoring the footpath to the left, continue into the next field and up round the edge to a kissing gate. From here there is an extensive view towards Bollington and Lyme Park, while White Nancy shows as a distant gleam on Kerridge Hill.

A cobbled path leads in front of a house then, turning left by the 16th century old hall, you pass the grand wrought iron gates of Legh Hall, built two centuries later. Crossing the busy Wilmslow Road, take the track opposite down past Hunter's Pool, then at the T-junction you go left, through Hunter's Pool Farm which dates from 1722.

The farm drive leads back to the A538, where a footpath turns right and heads straight across the fields. On reaching the lane, go right, then after passing the mellowed brick Withinlee Farm, a signpost points left through a holly hedge just before the next house. Follow the field edge down to cross a wooded clough, then emerging into the fields you join the track from Springsett Farm. In a few yards, a small gate leads onto the drive of Crabtree Cottage and this brings you to Chelford Road.

Go left for 100 yards and over a stile into the fields, and ahead in the distance is the flat-topped Shutlingsloe. Keep straight on down the field edge to a stone slab bridge, then slanting left a grassy track leads to a stile by a gate. Turning right and then left, you follow the hedge into Big Wood.

After descending to cross Spencer Brook,

Prestbury Village

the path climbs out of the wood. Take the stile opposite, onto Prestbury Golf course, and then turn right along the edge of the next field, but before reaching Fallibroome Farm, stiles lead left

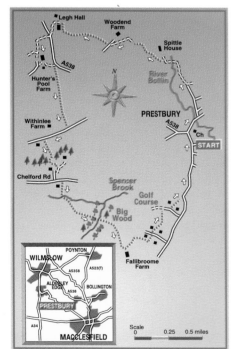

to King's School playing field. The way then goes left, round the field and out to a tarmac road. A path opposite leads between the gardens then, reaching the golf course again, way-marks point through the trees.

Joining the clubhouse road (watch for cars), turn right, then just past the first house go left over a stile and down to join the main road back into Prestbury.

The Old Hall, Prestbury

47

SIT ON HARRISON FORD

The Strid

LOCATION: 6 miles east of Skipton

START: Bolton Abbey village car park, off A59, toilets

DISTANCE: 6 miles (or 2½ if turning back at Cavendish Pavilion)

GRADE: Easy

TIME: 3 hours

MAP: Outdoor Leisure - Yorkshire Dales South, Landranger 104

REFRESHMENTS: Cavendish Pavillion

There was an autumnal haze in the air, the trees were just turning colour, and Bolton Abbey, in the heart of Wharfedale, looked at its very best. The gaunt Priory stood out majestically, ripples spread in widening circles as trout leapt for drowsy flies and paths led temptingly into the mysterious depths of the woods. This is a beautiful valley, and though perhaps best avoided on summer weekends, there is still peace and solitude to be found, while the river, as it falls in tumult through the polished rocks of the Strid, is one of the wonders of Wharfedale.

THE ROUTE

Follow the signs to the Priory into Bolton Abbey village and go through the Hole in the Wall. It is a dramatic entrance as you look down on the Priory, founded by the black-robed Augustinians in 1154, and though Henry VIII did his usual, thoroughly destructive job, the ruins are still magnificent.

Steps lead down across the parkland, past depressions which were medieval fishponds, then reaching the River Wharfe at the stepping stones you cross the footbridge. A good gravel path slants up the hillside, and continues above the river through mature beech, oak and ash. Meeting the road at Pickles Beck, with its choice of ford or footbridge, a path goes left through the river meadows. Then reaching Wooden Bridge, by Cavendish Pavillion where there is an excellent cafe, the Short Route turns back.

Continuing straight on, the path climbs a little by the rapids at Lud Stream Islands, and you follow the lower path through the trees. The road is met again at Posforth Bridge, and crossing the adjacent footbridge you enter Strid Wood, the largest acidic oakwood in the Dales National Park.

As the dark, still waters of Mason Holme Deep come into view, the path joins the river again, before climbing to Harrison's Ford Seat, an attractive stone shelter. Several minor paths lead down towards the river, but staying on the main path you contour the hillside through the beech trees high above the rocky gorge.

Emerging from the wood, the path continues to the castellated Victorian Aqueduct and, crossing over, the way now doubles back. Entering the trees, keep to the main path past High Strid with its weirdly sculpted rocks, and stay on the upper path until, just before the shelter at Lady Harriet's Seat, you turn down to the Strid. The 30ft deep gorge is carved out of millstone grit, but the rocks can be very slippery, so take care.

The Wheelchair Route, once the main carriageway through the woods, now leads along the dale. In about half a mile, there is a stone chair

Stepping stones by Bolton Priory

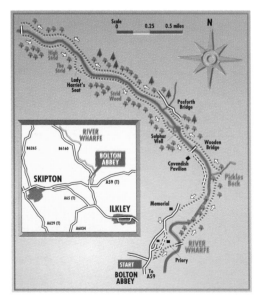

carved from a rock and, a similar distance beyond, after climbing the hill, you can detour left down some steps to visit the Sulphur Well, where a deep breath is a kill or cure remedy!

Re-joining the main path, you come to the 19th century Cavendish Pavillion. Stay beside the river, where dippers bob amongst the stones then, reaching the end of the car park, a path leads up to the Cavendish Memorial Fountain. A footpath beside the road re-enters the parkland at the bend, and keeping straight on past Bolton Hall, the Duke of Devonshire's private residence, it is only a short way back to Hole in the Wall and the village.

PRETTY AS A FIXTURE

LOCATION: 3 miles east of Chorley, off the road to Rivington

START: White Coppice, parking on unsurfaced road beyond village (please do not park at the cricket club)

DISTANCE: 4 miles

GRADE: Moderate

TIME: 2 hours

MAP: Explorer - West Pennine Moors, Landranger 109 & 103

REFRESHMENTS: Pack a flask

White Coppice cricket ground

Famed for its cricket ground, the prettiest in all Lancashire, the hamlet of White Coppice, near Chorley, was named after the white houses that once clustered round a cotton mill. Yet though the mill has long gone, the cottages are still whitewashed and the setting is delightful, for immediately above the green turf rise the steep slopes of the West Pennine moors. Then, as you climb away from the valley, the heather stretches for miles, while the views reach from the Lake District to the Welsh mountains.

THE ROUTE
Continuing up the rough track from White Coppice past the lodge, you come to the cricket ground with its white painted weavers' cottages. Go right, in front of the pitch, and after passing the pavilion, a bridge leads over The Goit, an aqueduct which links Anglezarke Reservoir with the higher Roddlesworth Reservoir.

Turning left a cobbled path then leads uphill past gritstone quarries that were busy in the 1920s. As height is gained, the view expands westward to encompass the Lancashire Plain and the sea, while on the moor a few stunted hawthorns struggle for existence, and to the south is the distant mast on Winter Hill.

The angle eases as a tumbled gritstone wall is reached by the ruins of Coppice Stile House, and to the left a fenced enclosure surrounds an old coal pit. Passing another ruined building, the path continues above the deep cleft of Dean Black Brook. Ahead rises the summit of Great Hill, while the clump of trees conceals the remains of the once substantial farm of Drinkwaters.

On reaching a T-junction, by a green signpost, you turn left on a rough track to Brinscall across Wheelton Moor. Here, small peaty pools have been made for the grouse, and on a good seeing day the landmark of Blackpool Tower is in view, while to the north Black Combe marks the end of the Lake District. Then, as the Forest of Bowland fells appear ahead, the Jubilee Tower on Darwen Hill stands on the eastern skyline.

Looking towards Great Hill

Continuing by a ruined wall, the track reaches the boundary of the Access Land and you turn left down a tarmac lane. After 100 yards, a wooden stile on the left leads into the field and, crossing to a ladder stile in the corner, you enter Wheelton Plantation. A faint path leads on for a few yards into the trees to join a clear, trodden path, and this heads downhill beside a ruined wall, through the forest of tall Scots pines and ancient beeches.

Turn left on reaching the main track, and keeping to this clear route, which climbs slightly to pass a ruin, it is easy walking beneath the canopy of ash and sycamore, oak, horse chestnut and beech. Gradually the path descends, then at the end of the wood you turn left over a stile onto the lower slopes of the open moor.

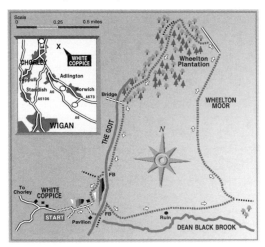

Going round to the left of the marshy area, a path follows the foot of the steep hillside through the bracken, then after half a mile joins an old sunken way to cross the bridge over The Goit. Although it was not introduced until 1839, the tall pink-flowered Himalayan Balsam, which flowers here in late summer, has now spread all over Britain. The path then veers left through the willows to a stile, and along the edge of the reservoir to a little gate and bridge into the cricket field.

51

POT LUCK

Pots and Pans

LOCATION: 6 miles east of Oldham

START: Binn Green car park on A635, toilets

DISTANCE: 3 miles (4½ miles via Alderman's Hill, but only do the extra if the weather is good)

GRADE: Moderate

TIME: 2 hours

MAP: Outdoor Leisure - Dark Peak, Landranger 110

REFRESHMENTS: Pack a flask

Apart from the sighing of the wind, all was quiet and still as we reached the Pots and Pans memorial. Beside the weathered gritstone tor, high on the Saddleworth Moors above Uppermill, the monument stood gaunt against the misty sky, and we looked out on a deserted landscape. But if you make the ascent on Remembrance Sunday, you will find the summit packed, for this is when people climb from the surrounding villages to hold a service on the hilltop.

THE ROUTE

Crossing the main road, follow the track slanting up the hillside. Soon Long Lane levels out and below to the left is Dovestone Reservoir, set amid encircling high moors, while closer at hand steep slopes rise to the craggy outline of Alderman's Hill.

Rounding a bend, the monument comes into view and you turn right through a gateway way-marked with the Oldham Way owl. Now the climbing begins in earnest. Speckle-faced sheep regarded us solemnly as we plodded up the hillside, while tumbled gritstone walls outlined ancient fields, and the gaping windows of Edge End recalled its days as a weavers' cottage.

Crossing a rush-filled track, the right of way follows a groove in the hillside, but later feet have taken an easier line. Then reaching the quarry, which has some interesting rock pillars, the path circles left.

Suddenly the angle relents and you reach the top. There is no mistaking the Pots and Pans Stone, but you will have to scramble up to see the scooped depressions after which it is named. Although people have rumoured that druids carved these circular depressions, it is simply the effect of wind and weather.

Just beyond, is the 50ft high obelisk, which was erected in 1923. It is a fine viewpoint, with the Tame Valley below. On the western skyline, you can make out Hartshead Pike and even Bishops Monument, while in every direction stretch the high moors.

If you feel like a further exploration before the descent, go through the gap in the railings and follow the Oldham Way. Descending a little, the path then climbs to the Sugar Loaf, an isolated rock just beyond an orange-topped pole. Although the track continues across the moor, our route now doubles back right on a faint grassy path, heading for Oven Stones.

Reaching this gritstone outcrop, the path disappears entirely, but 50 yards beyond, a narrow trod is joined on the edge of the moor. Turning left, it is then an easy stroll past Fairy Hole, a fissure to the left with reputedly 300ft of passages, which a group of schoolchildren were exploring on our visit.

Edge End

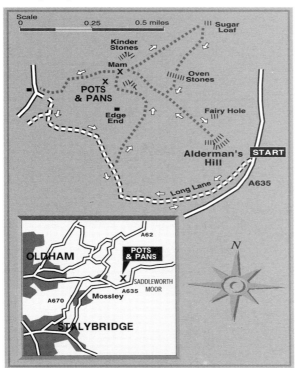

Arriving at the dramatic viewpoint of Alderman's Hill, a Celtic name meaning high rocks, it is a summit of which many a mountain would be proud. Retracing your steps, you follow the edge back to the monument. From the Uppermill side of the monument, a path heads down into the valley. It is a steep descent to a kissing gate, then squeezed between stone walls the way leads out to the road at Knowl Top Farm. Go left and immediately fork left along the track which contours the hillside. This is Long Lane, and rejoining the outward route, you continue back to the main road.

53

ENJOY A REAL LIFT

Anderton Lift

LOCATION: 2 miles north of Northwich
START: Marbury Country Park, signed from A533, toilets
DISTANCE: 4 miles
GRADE: Easy
TIME: 2 hours
BUS: From Northwich or Warrington: 46 (Mon-Sat only)
MAP: Pathfinder 758, Landranger 118
REFRESHMENTS: Anderton

Haunted by the ghost of an Egyptian princess who once lived here with her lover, Marbury Country Park, on the outskirts of Northwich, has a romantic appeal. It is a lovely setting beside Budworth Mere, with its winter colonies of golden eye and greylag geese, while in the woodland the great spotted woodpecker can be seen. After an easy stroll along the Trent and Mersey Canal, you arrive at the Anderton Boat Lift. A miracle of Victorian engineering, which linked the canal to the River Weaver, the gaunt frame has been slowly crumbling away, but now with Lottery funds it is being restored.

THE ROUTE

From the car park, walk past the Rangers Office and keep straight on down to the boathouse. Marbury, which means 'a fortified dwelling by a lake', was the name of the family that settled here in the 12th century and, though Marbury Hall itself was demolished 30 years ago, the two long avenues of lime trees are remnants of the original parkland.

Turning right along the Mere Side Path, which was created for the views across the lake to Great Budworth, you reach the old slipway. The path then continues through the trees past a stone-walled pit, the remains of an ice house where ice from the nearby pond was stored before the days of refrigerators.

The broad path leads through the fine old oaks, sycamores and beeches of Big Wood, then keeping left at the junction you follow Forge Brook. It was near here that the first rock salt in Britain was discovered in 1670, when prospecting for coal.

Meeting the Trent and Mersey Canal, continue along the path to Post 15 where a narrow trod leads left out to Marbury Lane, once a private toll road. Watch for cars as you cross the bridge, then joining the towpath you go under the bridge to follow the broad canal. Beyond the little white cottage of Jacksons Turn, the road is met briefly, then continuing along the towpath past the Anderton Marina, with its colourful rows of neatly moored narrow boats, you come to the Anderton Boat Lift.

The massive structure is best seen from below and a path leads down to the banks of the River Weaver for a closer view of the 50ft high pillars. The lift, which worked on a hydraulic system, was built in 1875, but has been out of use for 18 years.

Lime tree avenue

After continuing along the canal, climb up and cross the next bridge, which has been widened to take the modern road. Keeping right at the T-junction, take the broad grassy footpath in 100 yards on the left.

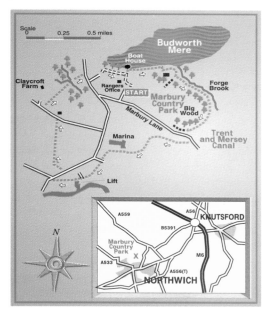

With a view of the Peak District hills, the path goes diagonally across the fields following a series of way-marked stiles, and on this section wintering redpolls and redwings, fieldfares and siskins may be seen. Reaching Cogshall Lane by the house, you turn left, then just before the entrance to Claycroft Farm, take the stile on the right.

Crossing the fields into Kennel Wood, continue over the lattice footbridge and out to the road. Turn right for a few yards, then go left down the drive to Marbury Hall Nursery. Keeping straight on, the concrete track leads past the green lawns of the demolished Marbury Hall and back to the Ranger Centre.

RIP SNORTER

Looking down on Ripponden

LOCATION: 5 miles north of Junction 22 on M62

START: Ripponden. Parking behind Conservative Club, toilets

DISTANCE: 4 miles

GRADE: Moderate

TIME: 2 hours

NOTE: Can be wet in places, wear boots or wellingtons

BUS: From Oldham: 562

MAP: Outdoor Leisure - South Pennines, Landranger 110 & 104

REFRESHMENTS: Ripponden

With Yorkshire's oldest inn and the longest single-span packhorse bridge in Calderdale, Ripponden presents a picturesque scene. Dating from the start of the 14th century, the town grew up at the meeting of several old ways by a ford over the River Ryburn. In 1881, the railway arrived. There were grand plans of continuing westwards, tunnelling beneath the moors into Lancashire, but this was the end of the line. Yet ancient cobbled paths still climb the steep wooded slopes, while on the old railway track, now reclaimed by nature, you stroll beneath a canopy of beech trees.

THE ROUTE

From the car park, cross the main road and follow the cobbled Priest Lane downhill past the whitewashed Bridge Inn. Crossing the ancient packhorse bridge, rebuilt in the 18th century after a flood, you continue past the Victorian church and follow the road which zigzags up the hill. It is a stiff ascent until, after passing Hanging Stones Lane and ignoring the next signpost left, you turn left just before reaching the fields on a level footpath into the trees.

The path contours the hillside between stone walls and continues across an open heathery area with a bird's eye view of the Ryburn Valley. Still on the level, the path goes through an ancient beech wood and on across the top of another field to a very tight squeezer stile. Crossing an old green lane, you continue in the same direction across the hillside following the walls until, after a rather muddy section, you turn right up the overgrown Highlee Lane.

Gorse bushes crowd the slope, then after briefly joining the Calderdale Way, you turn left on the footpath to Longley. The outcrop of Ladstone Rock on Norland Moor can be seen outlined against the sky, and you follow the wall down to Highlee Clough, but take care as the gritstone slabs over the brook are very slippery.

Entering Rough Hey Wood, don't go downhill, but take the higher path along the top edge to a stile. Then turning immediately left along the open hillside, you climb a little to follow an airy trod beneath the wall. The path leads into a beech wood and you take the lower

Bridge over the Ryburn Valley railway

route through the trees. A holly wood follows and, after wriggling through the bushes, the path crosses a field to the gritstone cottages at Longley.

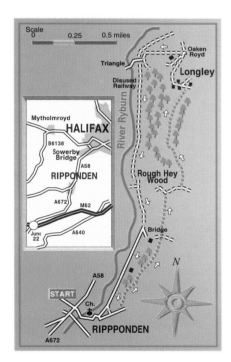

With Sowerby Bridge ahead in the valley, follow the cobbled lane between the houses and down the hill. Forking right, the track continues down to the isolated house at Oaken Royd and then doubles back beneath as a green lane.

Reaching a tarmac road, you cross the disused Ryburn Valley Railway and ahead lies the hamlet of Triangle, with its mill and cricket club. But turning left, a track leads down to join the disused railway, which closed in 1958.

The River Ryburn, the main tributary of the River Calder, is now a close companion and the railway provides easy walking through the woods. A mossy cutting, with high rock walls, is spanned by an asymmetrical bridge, then after a mile, at the next bridge, you leave the disused line.

Crossing the bridge, continue beside the railway along Hanging Stones Lane which, after climbing a little, continues past Far Hangingstones Farm. Then passing the new bungalows, the outward route is rejoined and you turn downhill back into Ripponden.

DON'T BE VAGUE...

The stone lion

LOCATION: 2 miles north of Wigan, well signposted from main roads

START: Haigh Country Park car park, toilets

DISTANCE: 4 miles (Red Trail, 2 miles)

GRADE: Easy

TIME: 2 hours

BUS: From Wigan 617

MAP: Pathfinder 711 & 712, Landranger 108 & 109

REFRESHMENTS: Haigh Hall cafe

Walking through the attractive woodland of Haigh Country Park on the fringe of Wigan, it is hard to believe that this was once the scene of a dreadful battle. Here, on the slopes of Monks Hill, the Royalists were defeated during the Civil War and the area is still called the Bloody Mountains. But now beech trees cloak the hillside, the Leeds and Liverpool Canal, which served the coalmines, is cruised by pleasure boats, while the stately Haigh Hall Estate, once the home of the Earls of Crawford, can be enjoyed by all the people.

THE ROUTE

Make your way across to the Haigh Information Centre and cafe and go round to the far side. Then going past the children's play area, follow the signs to the Woodland Trails. The trails are way-marked and, passing a carved stone lion, our route starts by following the green and red markers.

The gravel path leads through the rhododendrons and you keep straight on across the miniature railway and past the Swan Pond. This pool, so named because swan mussels were bred here, is now the home of the rare Great Crested Newt. Turn left at the crossroads and cross the railway again, then passing the gamekeeper's lodge you leave the track to follow a way-marked footpath straight on into the trees.

Reaching the edge of the wood, turn right on a track, the route of a former railway, and this leads down to cross the Leeds and Liverpool Canal where you turn right along the broad towpath. The fields here are reclaimed land which was once an opencast quarry. Reaching an ornamental bridge, the Red Trail crosses back into the park, but the longer Green Trail turns left, following the tarmac drive into Haigh Upper Plantation.

After the bend, fork left along a broad gravel path. These tall beeches, where busy grey squirrels dart to and fro, were planted in the 1860s. The path then loops round to rejoin the tarmac and crosses a disused railway line. The bridge was built good and wide so his lordship would not be troubled by steam from the trains.

Follow the tarmac into the Lower Plantation, then just before the hairpin bend a way-mark points off right. The narrow path contours

Haigh Hall

Monks Hill beneath tall sycamores with their flaky bark, then turns sharp right above the River Douglas. This valley was the site of the Battle of Wigan Lane in 1651, when the Earl of Derby was defeated.

Crossing a little clough, where a waterfall can be seen through the trees, turn right at the junction and follow the Green Trail uphill. Then 50 yards past a large quarry, watch for an indistinct stepped path where you turn left.

Emerging onto a track, you pass the mellowed stone almshouses, now private dwellings, and continue to Hall Lane. Turn right and, crossing the disused railway again, follow the tarmac lane past the houses, then turn left along a grassy track by a field gate. This bends right, and with Haigh Hall in view ahead, leads straight up to the canal.

Turning right along the towpath, you cross a little humpback bridge, until reaching the ornate canal bridge go over this to rejoin the Red and Green Trails. At the bend, leave the tarmac track to fork left through ancient beech trees and rhododendrons, until meeting the tarmac drive, you turn left back to Haigh Hall.

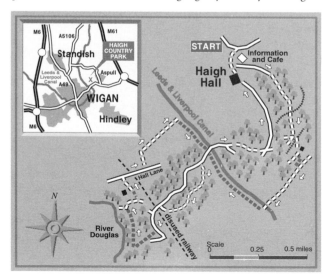

A WALK TO CROW ABOUT

LOCATION: 4 miles north of Oldham

START: Brushes Clough car park, off the B6197 by Shore Edge Chapel

DISTANCE: 3 miles

GRADE: Moderate

TIME: 1½ hours

BUS: From Manchester: 181 & 182

From Stalybridge: 408

MAP: Outdoor Leisure South Pennines & Pathfinder 713, Landranger 109

REFRESHMENTS: Pack a flask

Crompton Moor

Despite an encouraging forecast, the mist swirled about us as we climbed towards Crompton Moor, near Oldham; the trees were just grey shadows and Crow Knowl was invisible in the gloom. Muttering rude remarks about Michael Fish, we had a prolonged coffee break in the shelter of the larch plantation. Then, suddenly the mist was gone. Above us white clouds scudded across a blue sky, and the view stretched from the Peak District hills to Moel Fammau. We strolled on across the moor and ate our sandwiches with the sun sparkling on the surface of Brushes Clough Reservoir. Then, as we got back to the car, the heavens opened and it poured with rain all the way home.

THE ROUTE

Starting from the viewpoint at Brushes Clough Quarry, take the bridleway which climbs to the left of the quarry and fork right, round the top of the cliffs. This is the route of the Crompton Circuit, which encircles the town of Shaw, and also the Oldham Way.

A broad grassy ride leads up between the larch trees, and you keep straight on up the hill. Once this moor was colliery wasteland, and the quarry stone was crushed for moulding sand, but an EEC grant has improved the habitat for moorland birds, and meadow pipits now breed here.

Ignoring the stile ahead, follow the main path as it bends right along the top of the plantation, then turn left at the junction. The track leads along the hillside to a gate, where you fork left to climb past the spoil tip of an old coal mine, one of the 16 that covered the moor in the 19th century.

A narrow path continues up to join a track and, now reunited with the Crompton Circuit, you turn up the slope to a way-marked wooden stile. Passing another old coal mine, with its scrubby trees and encircling fence, the climb continues to the summit of Crow Knowl. Two substantial masts, and a third, anorexic companion, share the top with an OS trig point, a substantial

White painted stile

wind shelter, and a topograph. This 1286ft hill has recently been purchased by the local authority and is now safe from further development.

From a stile beyond the trig point, a faint path goes down to re-join the track. Turn left and follow it to the bend, where you go right through a small gate, still on the Crompton Circuit. Staying beside the wall and fence, the sunken way, a prehistoric trackway, leads round the edge of Crompton Moor until, after nearly a mile, with the Denshaw Valley far below, a small gate is reached.

Fork right into the dip, and go right to follow the tumbled wall down to the ruins of Higher Whitehill. Keeping above the ruins, go right into the next field and cross the boggy clough high up before heading down to a white painted stile. Continue in the same direction to another ruin, then follow the wall downhill to a wooden walkway by the remains of Bowling Green Farm. This 18th century farm was, like the rest, abandoned over 100 years ago when the reservoir was built.

The broad path then leads down past Brushes Clough Reservoir. Originally built to provide drinking water it is no longer used and the level was lowered a few years ago. After passing the reservoir, a little path turns right into Brushes Clough Quarry and so back to the car park.

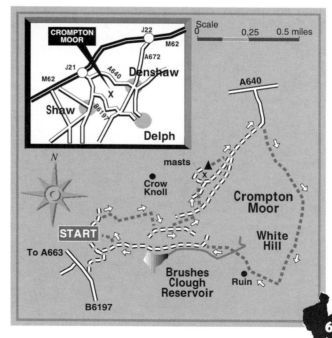

A SLICE OF LYME

Lyme Hall

LOCATION: 6 miles south east of Stockport
START: Lyme Park, off A6. NT car park, toilets
DISTANCE: 4 (or 2) miles
GRADE: Easy
TIME: 2 hours
NOTE: NT Lyme Hall open April-Oct.
Tel: 01663 766492
BUS: From Stockport: 361 & 199
MAP: Outdoor Leisure - Dark Peak,
Landranger 109
REFRESHMENTS: Lyme Hall

Ever since Mr Darcy went for that swim and Elizabeth gazed at the magnificent hall, Lyme Park has enjoyed an unexpected popularity, for this was the setting of Pemberley during the filming of *Pride and Prejudice*. You don't have to be a Jane Austen fan, however, to appreciate Lyme, for as well as the stately 18th century mansion and formal gardens, there are miles of footpaths, attractive woods and extensive views. The 1400 acre moorland park has a wild beauty of its own and the park is home to herds of red and fallow deer.

THE ROUTE

From the far end of the car park, follow the tarmac track up the hill then, just before the top of the rise, fork left along a grassy path above the stream. Passing a small plantation, you continue to the wall corner where a high stile leads into Pursefield Wood.

A path snakes up the hill through sycamore, oak and pine trees, and reaching the ridge the view opens out. This is the route Mr Darcy followed on his white horse back to Pemberley, while down to the left is the pool where he had his famous swim.

At the 17th century Paddock Cottage, recently restored by the National Trust, you double back down the lower grassy path through the pine trees. Then high above Poynton Brook, the path follows the tall gritstone wall along the rim of the steep-sided valley until, after a little footbridge, steps lead over the wall into Knightslow Wood.

Turn right and follow the path which stays beside the wall with extensive views over the deer park. The red deer stags and hinds live in separate groups, except in autumn when they come together at the 'rut'. Reaching a broad track, the Short Route turns left, before forking right to a gate at the top of the Lime Avenue.

However, the longer route crosses the ladder stile beside the gate and continues beside the wall on the edge of the moor. Arriving at the wall corner, you turn right and follow the wall uphill to a ladder stile into Lantern Wood. Passing above the tower, erected in 1729 on what was then open hillside, the path continues through the trees to another ladder stile.

As the path slants down across rough grass grazed by Highland Cattle, there is a good view of the Cage on the opposite hillside. The building, which dates from 1520, once housed the male servants. Crossing a stile in the fence near the gate, you turn left along the tarmac track. Soon Lyme Hall comes into view, but just before reaching the stable block, you turn left through a tall gate.

Red deer stags

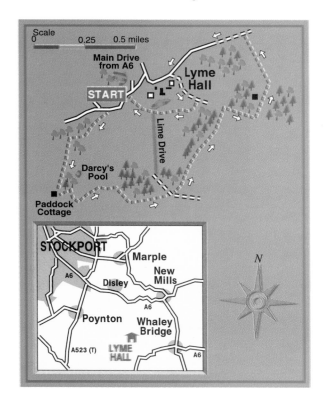

The track curves round to the right and, staying beside the garden fence, you turn right through a gate into the Fallow Deer Sanctuary. Although there have been fallows at Lyme for centuries, the numbers declined after the war and the deer were reintroduced in 1981.

Keeping right there is the classic view of the house, and the lawn where Elizabeth and Darcy met: then leaving the deer sanctuary, you rejoin the short route at the end of the Lime Avenue. This has been a feature of the park since the 17th century, and from here the path leads back into the car park.

MONUMENTAL MOOR

Peel Tower

LOCATION: Ramsbottom, 3 miles north of Bury

START: Holcombe Brook, park by shops on B6214 at junction with A676

DISTANCE: 4 miles

GRADE: Strenuous

TIME: 2 hours

BUS: From Bury: 474

NOTE: Not advised in mist. Tower occasionally open. Tel 0161 253 5899

MAP: Explorer - West Pennine Moors, Landranger 109

REFRESHMENTS: Holcombe & Ramsbottom

The ground was covered in snow and there was a Christmas feel to the air as we climbed from Ramsbottom towards Holcombe Moor and the Peel Monument. Peel was, of course, Sir Robert Peel, the founder of the police force, but he didn't get his memorial just for that. And he might not have got one at all, when you realise he was the first Prime Minister to introduce Income Tax in peacetime! But in 1846, he abolished the Corn Laws. These were a kind of price-fixing, which had kept bread prices high, so the monument commemorates not only a great statesman, but also a man who was a friend of the people.

THE ROUTE

From the traffic lights, head uphill a few yards and then turn right along the unsurfaced road beside the off-licence. After some terraced houses the road ends and a footpath sign points on beside the fields. Passing Redisher Farm, a track is joined which leads down into Redisher Wood. Don't cross the wooden bridge, but take the path to the left. This then crosses Holcombe Brook and, keeping to the lower fork, you continue up the valley.

After passing a dry hollow (all that remains of a former mill lodge), the path forks right and begins to climb. Emerging into the open, where stone gateposts mark the site of Lower Ridge Farm, you turn left along the grassy ridge. To the left is an army rifle range and also ITV's Krypton Factor assault course, but though MOD signs say that troops train here, fortunately it is outside the range and also a right of way.

The path forks at a grassy knoll, and going right descends past the ruins of Higher Ridge Farm and across the shallow valley to a stile into Saplin Wood. At first the path is rather indistinct, but heading straight up the slope it becomes clearer and brings you to a stile into the fields. It is a steady uphill plod over the grass to reach a gate beside the ruins of Taylor's Farm.

On Holcombe Moor

Now you turn left along the track, and ahead is a splendid view of Holcombe Moor, most of which belongs to the National Trust. Reaching the next ruin, where a couple of sycamores stand sentinel beside the remains of Hamlets Farm, leave the track to fork right up a clear path. Climbing steadily, you gain height until, meeting a stream, the path follows it up and suddenly the top of the moor is reached.

Rough tussocky mat-grass and heath rush stretch before you, but heading south west, a fair path crosses the moor and soon the tower appears. Harcles Hill Farm comes into view, then reaching the far side of the moor you turn right on a path leading directly to the Peel Monument. The tower, which is 128ft high, was built from stone quarried from the nearby pit, and was located here so that it could be seen by the owner of Nuttall Hall in the valley below.

Turn right along the track, which leads to Top o'th'Moor Farm, then follow it downhill. Rounding a bend at the bottom of the hill, you go left at the T-junction and then right on the cobbled road.

Descending gradually the old coach road from Bury to Haslingden crosses a minor road and continues down past the former sanatorium, now an Islamic College. Then reaching the bottom of the hill you turn left and out to the main road.

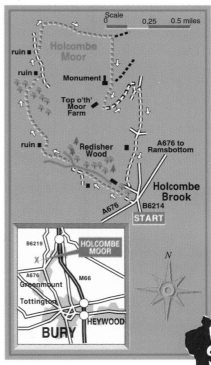

A MERE DEER STROLL

LOCATION: 12 miles south of Manchester

START: Knutsford station, parking by the station or in the town, toilets

DISTANCE: 4 miles

GRADE: Easy

TIME: 2 hours

NOTE: Tatton Park is open 11am-5pm, but closed Mondays during winter

BUS: From Altrincham 289 (& 288 via Wilmslow (not Sun))

TRAIN: Knutsford

MAP: Pathfinder 740 & 758, Landranger 109 & 118

REFRESHMENTS: Knutsford

King Street Knutsford by night

'A man is so in the way in the house!' observed one of the genteel maiden ladies of Cranford, which the author Mrs Gaskell modelled on Knutsford. And perhaps as you walk up the main street, you can still sense this refined matriarchy. Certainly Knutsford, which is named after King Canute, is holding back the tide of the 20th century, for along King Street the houses and hostelries long predate Mrs Gaskell. Then, leaving the town you step into Tatton Park, and here too the past remains, with red and fallow deer roaming beside a stately mere.

THE ROUTE

After walking down the station approach, turn left along King Street, the original main road through the town: 17th century cottages nudge you off the pavement, and the Georgian church is where Mrs Gaskell was married in 1832. A tall tower commemorates the famous author, while the Royal George pub is so old that nobody knows its age. then reaching the end of the street, where a glance down Drury Lane reveals the Italianate architecture of the Ruskin Rooms, you fork right along the track to Tatton Park.

The Doric arch at the entrance was designed by Lewis Wyatt who also built the hall and, bearing right through a small car park, a path leads by some fine mature beech trees and down over the grass to Tatton Mere. Herds of deer graze contentedly in the park, which was landscaped by Humphrey Repton at the end of the 18th century, while out on the lake, a black shape perched on a stake may be a cormorant.

Passing a group of tall Scots pine, the path hugs the lake shore, with its fringe of soft rush, and as we approached, a heron flapped lazily into the air. In the distance, Tatton House, which was built in the 19th century for the Egerton family, comes into view among the trees beyond

Melchett Mere. This mere, which was formed by salt extraction subsidence, is named after Lord Melchett who owned the mines.

At the head of the lake, where coots scurried busily about, flocks of black-headed gulls swarmed on the water and two swans circled their still brown cygnets. Then, after briefly joining the tarmac track, you turn right to continue along the eastern shore.

The gravelled track soon ends and a grassy path continues to a small gate in the fence beside a larch plantation. Gradually the path diverges from the lake and, joining a track, continues beneath

Swan patrolling the mere at Knutsford

magnificent sweet chestnut trees with their characteristic sawtooth edged leaves.

Reaching a tall gate in the high deer fence, you leave the restricted part of the estate to continue through Dog Wood. Eventually the path emerges from the trees at a stile, but don't cross the railway bridge. Instead, fork right, down across the rough grass, to enter the willow and alder carr.

A path comes in from the right, then in 50 yards you bear right down into a dip, through the trees and past a pumping station.

Reaching the Moor pool and reed bed, you turn right and up into the town where every Christmas a warm glow of fairy lights and decorated windows tempt the end of year shoppers.

WHERE THE GORGE RISES

Frosted spider's web

LOCATION: 3 miles east of Hyde
START: Lymefield Information Centre, Broadbottom, toilets
DISTANCE: 4 miles
GRADE: Moderate
TIME: 2 hours
NOTE: Visitor Centre open 12noon-4pm, Sat, Sun, Wed & Thu
BUS: From Manchester: 201 (Sun). From Hyde: 399
TRAIN: Broadbottom
MAP: Outdoor Leisure - Dark Peak, Landranger 109
REFRESHMENTS: The Waggon

Once, Roman soldiers, following a secret sunken path, crept unobserved from their fort at Melandra up to a look-out post high above Longdendale. It is a marvellous vantage point, and climbing from Broadbottom near Hyde, where the River Etherow flows in its steep-sided gorge, old packhorse ways and paths lead up through ancient woodland. Then reaching Mottram church, which stands sentinel on the top of the hill, you look out like a centurion with a view far over the surrounding countryside.

THE ROUTE

Turn left down the track by the Visitor Centre, then go right in front of Lymefield Terrace where a kissing gate leads onto the site of Broad Mills. Once employing around 2000 people, this was the largest cotton mill in the area and there are several interesting interpretation boards. The path then bends left by the engine house, down to the River Etherow.

Continuing through the sycamore trees, steps lead up to Warhurst Fold Bridge. Don't cross the river, but follow the path uphill and turn left along a rough cobbled track. This old packhorse way, which was used to transport Cheshire salt into the Pennines, leads high above the deep Broadbottom Gorge and past the weavers cottages of Summerbottom, which were built in the 1780s.

Hodge Lane goes down to meet the river again and passes the restored stone Dye Vats, where cloth was washed, bleached and dyed before being spread out in the adjacent field to dry. Keep straight on to Hodge Fold, with its 17th century agricultural cottages, then cross the stream and turn right. A short track leads to a flight of about 50 steps up into Great Wood, which dates back to at least 1600.

The narrow path climbs on through the trees, then crossing the railway bridge you turn immediately right beside the railway. The right of way leads into Hurst Wood and you go left on a path which follows the edge of the ravine. Descending to Hurstclough Brook, cross

68

the footbridge and climb the steps then, after crossing back over the stream, you turn left at the waymarked T-junction and continue up the valley.

Don't cross the next footbridge, but stay on the terraced path which keeps to the right of the brook. After a footbridge over a side valley, a stepped path climbs out into the open and you

Mottram Church from the secret way

walk up beside the trees to join Broadbottom Road opposite The Waggon.

To the left of the pub, a footpath leads across the fields, and then follows the fence to Littlemoor Road. Turning left along the lane, in half a mile you fork right to Mottram Church. The ornate sundial commemorates Queen Victoria's Diamond Jubilee and, from the gravestone-paved churchyard, you look down on Longdendale and the green space that once was Melandra.

Crossing the stile to the right of the school ('private' only refers to fishing), follow the wall round to meet a sunken lane which leads down to a small pool. Continue straight on, following the fence on the right, and the ancient hollow way reappears to lead down to the hamlet of Hague. Turn right on Pingot Lane and keeping right at the junctions you pass several attractive cottages.

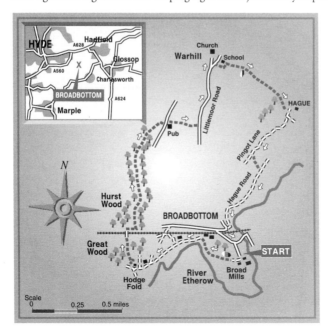

After going under the pylons, a way-marked path goes left and down beside the hedge to Hague Road.

Turning right, and past a grand mansion built by a cotton mill owner, the track leads to Gorsey Brow. Walk down to the main road, under the railway bridge, and back to the Visitor Centre.

COAL MINES & CANALS

LOCATION: Between Bolton and Manchester
START: Just off Junction 13 on M60. Car park
on B5211, opposite Worsley Court House, toilets
DISTANCE: 3 miles
GRADE: Easy
TIME: 1½ hours
BUS: From Manchester: 68
MAP: Pathfinder 712 & 723, Landranger 109
REFRESHMENTS: Worsley

Packet House & Bridgewater Canal, Worsley

'Illiterate man in charge of the Tunnel!' You can just imagine the headlines if someone today discovered that the Chief Engineer could neither read nor write. But when it came to the Duke of Bridgewater's mines at Worsley, he was impressed by deeds, not paper qualifications. James Brindley had conceived a most original idea. Coal mines suffer from too much water, while canals frequently have too little. So why not extend the canal right into the workings? It was a sensational advance, yet this brilliant engineer left not a word or a drawing of his work.

THE ROUTE

Crossing straight over the B5211, go down to the canal, which is stained a bright orange by iron deposits from the coalmines. Passing the Packet House, a footbridge leads left, where Muscovy ducks look hopefully for food, and you follow the stepped path up by the white house out to Worsley Road.

Take great care crossing. On the far side is the Delph canal basin, hemmed in by a sandstone cliff, and at its base are two tunnel entrances where barges brought out the coal from the mines. The Bridgewater Canal, which opened from Worsley to Stretford in July 1761, was the first major undertaking of the canal era, while the underground waterways totalled an incredible 52 miles.

Walking past the shops you turn left up Mill Brow and, reaching the top, a track continues into Worsley Woods. Huge beech trees overlook Old Warke Dam, where coots, tufted duck, swans and great crested grebe can be seen. The pool was built by damming Kempnough Brook to provide fishing for the duke, who also built the black and white house on the far side as a hunting lodge. The woods, which extend up to and beyond the motorway, were planted to give employment to mill-workers during the 19th century cotton famine.

Reaching the half-timbered house, take the right fork and keep straight on to a flight of steps down to the disused Tyldesley Loopline, where you turn right. Here we met a barn owl. Born in a bird sanctuary to parents who would never fly again, he could not be released into the wild, but returned happily to his owner's wrist after exploratory flights into the surrounding trees. A short tunnel takes you under Worsley Road and the tree-lined track continues past the platform of Worsley Station, which opened in 1864. The line, linking Eccles to Wigan,

The Court House, Worsley

passes through Broadoak Park, then after a mile you come to Monton. The dark steeple of the Unitarian Church appears through the trees, and joining the road you turn right on Parrin Lane.

Passing the end of Duke's Drive, and its gatehouse with the tall chimneys, cross the canal and then turn immediately right to join the towpath. There are no navigation problems now, for the canal leads all the way back to Worsley. Arriving at the coal basin, where barges and boats lie moored, you pass The Granary and opposite are the Dry Docks which date from the early 1760s. Continuing along the canal, go under the road-bridge where a flight of steps leads up onto the road near the car park.

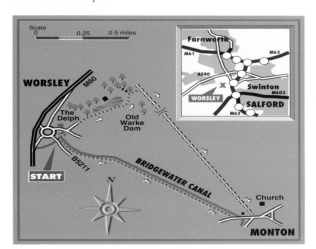

The barn owl

TRICKY DICKIE AND A LLAMA CALL

LOCATION: 2 miles south east of Whaley Bridge

START: Combs Reservoir, off B5470.

Parking beneath the dam

DISTANCE: 4½ (or 3) miles

GRADE: Moderate

TIME: 3 hours

NOTE: Can be muddy so don't forget your boots

BUS: From Stockport: 198 & 199

MAP: Outdoor Leisure - White Peak,

Landranger 119

REFRESHMENTS: Beehive Inn

Llama

It was all Dickie's fault, for when the railway bridge beside Combs Reservoir collapsed it was found that someone had moved his skull. Kept upon a bible at Tunstead Farm near Whaley Bridge, Dickie's Skull, which had belonged to a soldier, had a habit of causing mishaps when disturbed. However, the Buxton Railway prevailed in the end and separated Combs from its namesake lake. But as we strolled beside the reservoir looking for the tiny firecrest, a bird which is almost indistinguishable from the goldcrest (except by other firecrests!), we blamed its absence on the ghostly Dickie.

THE ROUTE

From the car park, cross the tarmac lane and follow the concrete path beside Combs Reservoir. This soon becomes a muddy strip, squeezed between Meveril Brook and the lake, which was built in 1799 to supply the Peak Forest Canal. Reaching the footbridge, don't cross, but stay beside the stream and continue along the embankment. After passing the end of the reservoir, you go over the single-rail footbridge to the left. The mysterious arrangement of streams here is explained by a weir which divides the flow.

Climbing the grassy bank, head for the distant escarpment of Castle Naze, a sandstone precipice defending an Iron Age fort. Crossing a rickety gate, go to the right of the barn and over a once important track which was severed by the railway. The next stile needs an athletic approach, then at the opposite corner of the field you join the road.

Turn right and under the railway, which was built 50 years after the reservoir, and follow the road into Combs village. Though the Methodist Chapel now has a service only twice a month, it doubles as the Primary school. Forking right at the Beehive Inn, you keep straight on past the miniature Post Office, with the tall television mast on Ladder Hill a prominent landmark. The tarmac lane leads gently uphill, then, after a brief flirtation with the railway, climbs steadily past Spire Hollins Farm with its fine mullioned windows.

As the tarmac turns away to Thorny Lee (so named when the ground was cleared of thorns in medieval times), you turn right on the unsurfaced track. Enclosed by gritstone walls and

Gulls on Combs Resovoir

edged with bilberry, the way continues round the hill, until from the gate at the highest point you look over Combs Reservoir to Eccles Pike, Chinley Churn, and the distant Kinder Scout. Here the Short Route turns back, crossing the stile beside the gate to descend a grassy path to Tunstead Farm.

After continuing along the airy track, it descends towards the long ridge of Taxal Moor. Reaching Elnor Lane, which was the Roman Road from Buxton to Manchester, you turn downhill until, after about 100 yards, a footpath sign points right. As we followed the wall round the hillside, the llamas in the next field glanced up as if to say "what strange animals!".

Reaching a gritstone step stile, stay by the wall and descend past the grassy mound of an empty reservoir. Then, after crossing a three-way stile, you turn right and follow the wall along the

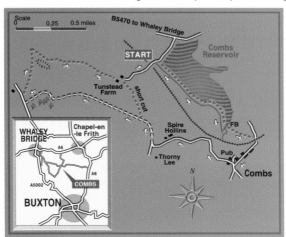

hillside. Passing a wooded clough, go down across the next field to a wire-festooned stile in the far corner. The path continues along the hillside, beneath the holly bushes and, becoming enclosed, leads to Tunstead Farm.

Taking the path to the right of the buildings, you join the tarmac lane which leads down to Dickie's Bridge and the reservoir.

73

MARTON'S HISTORY LESSON

Marton Church

LOCATION: 4 miles north of Congleton
START: School Lane off A34. Roadside parking in half a mile
DISTANCE: 4 miles
GRADE: Easy
TIME: 2 hours
MAP: Pathfinder 776, Landranger 118
REFRESHMENTS: Davenport Arms & Marton café

"We used to play spinning tops in the road," said the old gentleman who was born and bred in the village of Marton. Named after a long vanished mere, the community has a delightful little black and white church, the oldest European half-timbered church still in use, while its 600-year-old oak tree, with a trunk almost 50 feet in girth, is the largest in Cheshire. Marton's farms, too, have a history going back over many generations, but the children certainly don't play in the middle of the road any more.

THE ROUTE

Head away from Marton along School Lane then, after Pikelow Farm, you turn right on the unsurfaced Common Lane to Marton Heath Kennels. Passing a trout pool, which was created from damp meadows whose rushes were once cut to make hay, the track continues through Martonheath Wood where Capesthorne Estate pheasants scuttle under the rhododendrons and silver birch trees.

Beyond the kennels, you emerge from the wood and keep straight on along the track. Suddenly there is a splendid view of Croker Hill, crowned by the BT tower, with Shutlingsloe behind, while to the south is the scarp slope of the Cloud and the Mow Cop ridge.

The track continues past a fenced swamp, and on across the grassy fields to Great Tidnock Farm. The bridleway is signed through the farmyard, and beyond at the bend you turn right through the way-marked gate. At first the route follows the fence, where gritstone slabs cover an old well, then veering left you descend to the hedge which leads to a double-gated bridge over Chapel Brook.

Continue up the hill by the holly trees until, at the top of the field, you turn right over the stile and keep straight on to the far hedge. This leads up to Higher Mutlow, where a courtesy path goes left, past the tennis court, then skirts the garden to join the tarmac drive.

Passing a silver birch wood, you leave the tarmac at the bend and turn right through a field gate. The track beside the hedge leads to Mutlow Farm, where you keep left and follow the farm drive past Cocksmoss Wood, out to the lane where you turn right.

In 300 yards, a footpath sign points right, over the fields, to Marton. The path follows the line of the power cables and continues beside the hedge, with a distant view of the church of St James and St Paul. Reaching a double stile, the field boundary is

The Marton Oak

followed to a gate by a barn, and out to the main road at Chapel Bridge.

Turning right, it is an easy plod on the pavement up to the ancient church, which was founded in 1343. In the churchyard stands a Preaching Cross, which probably predates the building, and inside is a medieval stone font, a carved wooden pulpit, dating from 1612, and an Elizabethan wooden chest. During restoration, a wall painting of the Last Judgement, probably as old as the church itself, was discovered on the west wall.

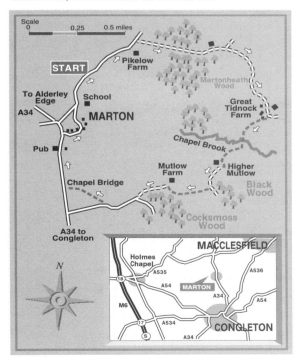

Next stop is Church Farm, where you can visit the animals, the craft workshops and farm shop, not to mention the cafe. Continuing past the Davenport Arms, you turn right down Oak Lane. This was named after the Marton Oak which, until it split into three, was the largest in England, and still has a girth of 44ft. Passing the primary school, you turn right at the T-junction onto School Lane.

HADES' WATERY GRAVES

Icicles in the quarry

LOCATION: 4 miles north of Rochdale

START: Trap Farm Car Park, Wardle, off A58

DISTANCE: 4 miles

GRADE: Easy

TIME: 2 hours

NOTE: Can be muddy

BUS: From Rochdale: 450, 455, 458, 700

MAP: Outdoor Leisure - South Pennines, Landranger 109

REFRESHMENTS: Pack a flask

Piles of gritstone blocks, that once were farms, lie tumbled on the hillside above Rochdale, and on the grassy slopes shaly mounds hint at long forgotten mines. This is a wild landscape where the sheep look up startled as you pass, for there is no-one else in view. Yet here stood the village of Watergrove, with 40 houses, a church, two pubs and two mills. But then the valley was flooded and now, as the wind sighs over the stones, only ghosts remain among the ruins while moorland is fast reclaiming the deserted hillside.

THE ROUTE

A flight of steps leads to the top of Watergrove Reservoir embankment, where you turn right. In the 1930s, the demand for water was so great that the valley was flooded and the village and surrounding farms demolished. But many of the datestones from the houses have been preserved, and reaching the end of the dam you turn left past the Wall of History where these are displayed.

Crossing the stream, which is fed by the Blue Pots Aqueduct from the far side of the hill, you go through a small gate to follow the path by the water's edge. At the modern Sailboard Club building, which stands on the site of Watergrove Mill, a cotton spinning mill, turn right up the cobbled Ramsden Road. Reassuring yellow arrows and an 'H' indicate the Hades Trail, and this is followed for the rest of the walk.

After passing the ruined cottages of Little Town, the track goes through a gate and climbs on gently across the grassy moor past the site of Steward Barn. Forking right, stay on the main track which, after a gateway, bends left. The ancient line of the Long Causeway, an old packhorse way, can be seen slanting up to the skyline on the right, and dotted across the hillside are the dark spoil heaps of drift mines. Though the coal was of poor quality, it was used by the local mills.

After passing a disused quarry, you come to a T-junction where a waymark points left across a moorland clough beside more old quarries, festooned with icicles on our visit. The track passes the ruins of Higher Slack, then curves on round the valley to a prominent spoil heap, where off to the right is the fenced entrance of the Hades Hill Aqueduct.

Seated by Watergrove Reservoir

Another pile of rubble marks Lower Hades, then immediately after the ruins you fork left and leave the main track. Yellow arrows indicate the way across the rough pasture and, crossing Calf Clough, you head towards four sycamores that stand guard over the ruins of Hades Farm.

Here an ancient grassy track is joined, and you continue past the ruins of Middle Hill to Long Shoot Clough and Broad Ing. After crossing the lower slopes of Brown Wardle Hill, a signpost, by a solitary sycamore, points left down a narrow walled lane to the ruins at High Wardle. Dating from 1646, this was the oldest building in the valley.

Keeping above the ruins, follow the sunken High Wardle Lane to a way-marked wooden stile. Turn left along the narrow walled lane, and this leads downhill until, reaching a gate, you go left to the Valve Tower. Then, crossing the overflow bridge, you walk back to the steps along the top of the embankment, with a view of Wardle Church's 19th century spire.

TAMING THE WITCH

LOCATION: 2 miles north of Stockport

START: Reddish Vale Visitor Centre, signed from B6167, toilets

DISTANCE: 5 (or 3½) miles

GRADE: Easy

TIME: 2½ hours

BUS: From Manchester: 203

TRAIN: Reddish South

MAP: Pathfinder 724, Landranger 109

REFRESHMENTS: Arden Arms

Arden Hall

The witch of Reddish Vale was most upset. The railway company had built a viaduct over the River Tame in her favourite valley. So, being a witch, she put a curse on it: seven years of bad luck would befall anyone who counted the number of arches. Well, the viaduct is still there, but the valley has been reclaimed to form a green oasis. Now herons flap lazily over the water meadows, and Hulmes Wood edges a clean, swift flowing stream. We are sure the witch would approve but, just in case, don't count the arches.

THE ROUTE

The walk starts from the Visitor Centre, where ducks and geese flock on ponds which once supplied a calico printing works. A black-railed bridge leads over the River Tame and, turning left, you follow the Reddish Vale Trail under the high arches of the railway viaduct. Men perched high on scaffolding were working on repairs as we passed, for the bridge was built in 1875.

Keep straight on along the good path, then fork left, signed Arden Hall. Staying down in the valley, a narrow tree-lined path skirts the water meadows beneath a wooded slope of willow trees. Ignoring paths that climb up to the tower blocks at Brinnington, you cross a stream to follow a wooded gully where, despite the proximity of the M60, birds rustle through the undergrowth. A wooden footbridge leads out to a playing field, where you go left, then left again across the motorway.

Going immediately left, a footpath leads round Bredbury Industrial Estate, and soon you are heading away from the motorway and past the turreted Arden Hall. Cromwell is reputed to have stayed here, though the present moated hall only dates back to the 18th century, replacing an earlier dwelling built in 1350.

Continue down Battle Lane, named from the Civil War, then turn left past the cottages at Castle Hill, the site of an ancient fortification. Emerging opposite the Arden Arms, the Short Route turns left along Stockport Road, but the longer route crosses straight over to the cobbled Arden Road.

After passing the cottages and a pool fished by Arden Anglers, the tarmac bends away and, following the unsurfaced Turner Lane across the fields, you feel in the heart of the country. In the distance is Werneth Low, then nearing a farm, you turn left down an ancient track to

Arden Bridge, which spans the river above a horseshoe-shaped weir.

Turn left along the Tame Valley Way then after a red sandstone quarry, a prettier path hugs the riverbank. Rejoining the main path, stay by the river through the wood, with its green-budded sycamores, to pass the site of Hulmes Pit, a coal mine which closed in 1929.

Reaching the main road, where the Short Route is rejoined, turn right up the hill, then go left after the red brick house. The path follows a boggy hollow and goes under a pipe. Staying down near the river, follow the way-marks to a stone stile and past the bulrushes, then the path goes under the motorway and over a board walk below Holt Wood.

The railway viaduct

Waymarks lead along the wooded slope to Ross Lave Lane, where you turn left and under the viaduct. Joining a track, you go left again and then right, between the fishing ponds, back to the Visitor Centre.

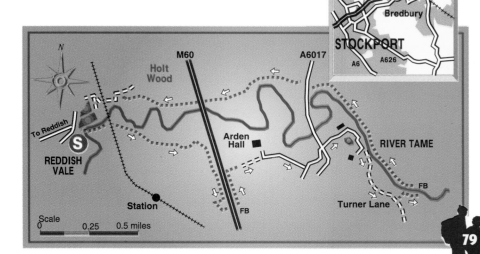

79

RESERVOIR TRODS

The Fairy Battery

LOCATION: 5 miles north of Bolton

START: Car park by reservoir dam off B6391

DISTANCE: 3½ miles

GRADE: Easy, with a short ascent that can be avoided

TIME: Up to 2 hours

TRAIN: Entwistle

MAP: Explorer - West Pennine Moors, Landranger 109

REFRESHMENTS: Pack a flask

The reeds were beaded with ice and only a few hardy mallards braved the freezing water of Turton and Entwistle Reservoir, near Bolton. A bitter wind blew through the trees and people slithered their way along the glassy path that surrounds the lake. But as we left the waterside to climb through the beechwood and out onto the hillside, the sun emerged. Basking in unexpected warmth, we ate our sandwiches by the ruins of an abandoned farm and looked out over the valley and the dark forest to the high moors beyond.

THE ROUTE

A gate, on the opposite side of the road from the car park, is the start of the circular walk round Turton and Entwistle Reservoir. The good path hugs the lake shore, with its fringe of reed canary-grass, and ahead lie the slopes of Turton Moor, while to the left are the larch and pines of Tarkingtons Plantation.

Reaching the end of the lake, don't cross the footbridges but stay beside the stone-pitched Cadshaw Brook, where small weirs slow the flow of the water to reduce the amount of silt carried into the reservoir. Then in about 400 yards, a flight of steps leads down to a footbridge opposite the Fairy Battery, a prominent rocky cliff above steep bracken-covered slopes. Now popular with rock climbers, this was a secret meeting place in the 17th century when non-conformists broke the law by coming here to worship.

Follow the stream back on the far side through the beech trees until you come to a stile at the forest corner. The easier option continues beside the brook to rejoin the reservoir perimeter path, but the more energetic route is well worth the extra effort for its spectacular views of the surrounding countryside.

Crossing the field, the path climbs the hill beside a grassy hollow, and then turns right, parallel to Fox Hill Plantation. Joining a wider track, you continue above the trees, and in the distance is the Peel Tower on Holcombe Moor.

At the end of the wood, there is the option of descending to join the perimeter path beside a carved totem pole, but the main route veers left across pathless grass to a stile into the wooded clough.

Descending to a small wooden footbridge, you climb through the beech trees, trending left to emerge over a stile into the fields. Continue gently climbing, following the edge of a clough until, after passing an isolated gritstone gatepost, you veer left to join a track at a stile by a gate.

The totem pole

Looking westwards, Winter Hill, with its cluster of masts, is now in view, but turning right you follow the track for 300 yards. At the bend, go right and down an old walled track under the beeches to the site of Burton Hill farm, abandoned in the mid-19th century when the reservoir was converted for drinking water.

The grassy track bends left across the field and down into the plantation to join the perimeter path where Entwistle Fly Fishers cast their lines into a reservoir built for the bleachworks, but which now supplies the thirst of Bolton.

Keeping straight on, you join the road by the dam, with its elephant and castle crest, and this leads back to the car park.

Fairy Battery

Edge Fold

ruin

Entwistle Station

Turton and Entwistle Reservoir

S

B6391

Edgworth

A666 B6391 RAMSBOTTOM

Egerton

Egerton A676 Bradshaw

BOLTON

N

Scale
0   0.25   0.5 miles

GOING BACK IN TAME

Roaches Lock pub

LOCATION: 3 miles north east of Stalybridge

START: Castle Clough car park at the end of Buckton Vale Road, off B6175

DISTANCE: 5 miles

GRADE: Moderate

TIME: 3 hours

BUS: From Manchester: 231-235. From Oldham: 343

MAP: Outdoor Leisure - Dark Peak, Landranger 109

REFRESHMENTS: Roaches Lock

From the gamekeeper's cottage, set beside a Roman road high above the River Tame, we looked down on the mist-filled valley - and were transported back to an era when the Industrial Revolution was cranking into gear. Below us was Stalybridge, one of the first industrial areas in the world. But now the mills are silent and, descending to the valley, we walked beside the Huddersfield Narrow Canal. Abandoned to boats long since, the waterway is being restored to celebrate the Millennium, while beside the River Tame, once a source of power for the mills, there are stoats, foxes and kestrels.

THE ROUTE

From the car park, follow Carr Rise up past the 19th century mill workers' houses, which cluster round the bowling green, and at the junction continue straight on up the hill. Above the cottages, the road ends and a path goes left to thread its way through the heather, beneath steep oak-clad slopes. Reaching the field, aim for a stile by the houses, and cross the quarry road to Castle Farm.

A rough track, appropriately known as Moor Edge Road, forks right and begins to climb before contouring the heather slope. High above is Buckton Castle, an ancient earthwork dating back to the 13th century, while across the valley stands the tower on Hartshead Pike, built in 1863 to commemorate the marriage of Edward VII.

The old road, which the Romans built to link Glossop with Castleshaw Fort, heads towards the distant point of Noonsun Hill, then dips to pass Intake Cottage and Micklehurst Brook. After joining the track from Greentop Farm, you fork right to pass the Stalybridge Estate gamekeeper's cottage, which looks down on the unusual glass tower of the Water Treatment Works.

Keeping to the higher track, carry on round the hillside until, as the Pots and Pans Memorial comes into sight, you turn left down Shadworth Lane. Crossing the B6175 by a Boundary Stone, which until 1974 marked the Lancashire/Cheshire boundary, you turn left along the sandy bridlepath, once the Stalybridge to Diggle railway line.

Immediately after a gate, turn right to descend through Roaches Wood to the Huddersfield Narrow Canal, which was opened in 1811. A little, white-painted bridge leads to Roaches Lock pub, then turning left you follow the towpath to the derelict Woodend Mill, whose loading gates can still be seen.

Crossing the canal, continue past the site of Milton Mill and on to Micklehurst. After the second road bridge, you leave the canal

Sculpture by the Huddersfield Canal

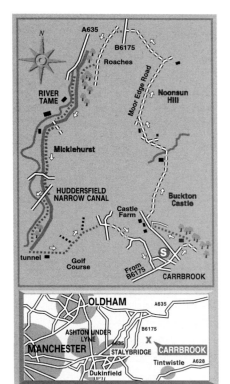

and double back across the bridge, before turning left on the track beside the River Tame. Stick to the path closest to the river, which rises high on the Pennine Moors above Denshaw, and follow it until suddenly you are reunited with the Huddersfield Canal.

As the canal disappears into Scout Tunnel, go left to the three storied Kershaw Hey Cottage. Then, keeping straight on to a signpost, turn left to cross the clough. A short ascent brings you to the churchyard wall with extensive views across the golf course to Buckton Moor and Harridge Pike.

Follow the wall round to the right and fork right at the corner out to Staley Road. Crossing the main road, you follow the cobbled Heyheads New Road and, keeping left, then left again, this leads back to the calico-printing village of Carrbrook.

GO WITH THE FLOW

The oval horse tunnel

LOCATION: 3 miles east of Stockport

START: Chadkirk Country Estate, off A627

DISTANCE: 6 miles

GRADE: Easy

TIME: 3 hours

NOTE: Chadkirk Chapel open most Sat and Sun afternoons

BUS: From Stockport; 358, 383

TRAIN: Marple or Rosehill

MAP: Outdoor Leisure - Dark Peak, Landranger 109

REFRESHMENTS: Marple

Water doesn't usually flow uphill, but at Marple Locks it comes pretty close, for in a distance of little more than a mile the canal climbs over 200ft. This stupendous achievement of 18th-century engineering included the magnificent 97 feet high Marple Viaduct and a 300 yard long tunnel, where bargees 'legged it', lying on their backs and pushing the barges along with their feet. After the Macclesfield Canal, with its ancient roving bridges, you walk along the Middlewood Way, where brightly coloured bullfinches flutter among the trees, and return over the fields by the wooded Marple Brook.

THE ROUTE

From the far side of the car park, take the footpath beside the stream. Soon this curves away from the main road, past an old sluice gate, a reminder that, until 1977, a bleaching, dying and printing works stood here. Then passing Little Wood, you go down the steps to Chadkirk Farm. The animals can be visited with the farmer's permission and Chadkirk Chapel, where St Chad founded a monastic cell in the 7th century, is just beyond.

A short climb up the tarmac road takes you past St Chad's Well and by Kirkwood Cottage, a former toll house. At the top of the hill, a flight of steps leads up to the Peak Forest Canal, where you go right. Passing Oakwood Mill, built in 1848 for cotton spinning, Hyde Bank Tunnel is reached and the path climbs away from the canal.

Turning right to pass Hyde Bank Farm, which was built by Robin Hyde who fought for Cromwell in the Civil War, you go right again to rejoin the canal. Now you are high above the river, on the Goyt Embankment, and the canal squeezes through a narrow defile which was once a tunnel.

Reaching Marple Aqueduct, which was rescued from demolition in the 1960s, there are splendid views of the Peak District framed by the arches of the railway. After going under the railway and crossing sides, the towpath begins to climb the flight of 16 locks. Soon the railway is far below and you reach Station Road. Continue on the far side, past the restored Oldknow's Warehouse, where a flight of steps leading down to the water was for collecting tolls.

At Posset Bridge, the towpath goes through the oval Horse Tunnel, while a narrow passage by the lock gate was for the boatmen. At Marple Junction, go over the Roving Bridge, designed so a horse could cross the canal without unhitching, then turn right along the Macclesfield Canal. Passing the All Weather Warehouse, where

Oakwood Mill

boats were handled under cover, you cross another Roving Bridge and follow the canal past the gaunt red brick Goyt Mill, a cotton mill which closed in 1960.

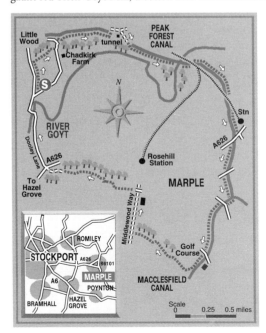

At the next bridge, you leave the towpath and the right of way follows an old banked hedgerow across the golf course to a wooded clough. Reaching the Middlewood Way, a former railway line, turn right, then in a quarter of a mile, and after passing a tall factory chimney, you climb the steps and cross the bridge.

A grassy track leads across the fields to a stile, then turning right you follow the hedge. Joining a track, keep straight on past Higher Danbank Farm, and follow the lane down to the main road. Crossing over, keep straight on down Dooley Lane, past the Hare and Hounds, back to Chadkirk Estate.

SALT' N' VIGOUR

Errwood Reservoir

LOCATION: Between Whaley Bridge and Buxton

START: Goyts Lane Car Park, off A5004

DISTANCE: 3½ (or 2) miles

GRADE: Moderate

TIME: 2 hours

MAP: Outdoor Leisure - White Peak, Landranger 119

REFRESHMENTS: Pack a flask

Smugglers once crossed the Goyt, near Whaley Bridge, their packhorses laden with salt, and climbed across the slopes of Wild Moor. It still feels wild as you follow the brook up into the hills, but suddenly there is a surprise. With its now deserted track contouring the slope, the Cromford and High Peak was one of the first railways in Britain. Then came the reservoirs, the old Salt Way was cut in half, and the farms abandoned. Now the only inhabitants are the speckle-faced Derbyshire Gritstone sheep, but this is where they belong, for the ancient name of the breed was Dale o'Goyt.

THE ROUTE

A few yards uphill from the car park, take the footpath which is signed down into the Goyt Valley. It is a gentle descent following a grassy path towards the distant blue patch of Fernilee Reservoir, completed in 1938, while, to the right, beneath the whaleback hump of Combs Moss, lie three separate routes to Buxton. The highest is the Roman Road, then comes the modern road, made in 1820, and below this is the walled track of Old Longhill Road, built by the famous Blind Jack of Knaresborough.

The path bends left to meet the steep metalled road, built on the Bunsal Incline of the Cromford and High Peak Railway, and crossing over you join the footpath along the hillside. Yellow arrows indicate the route over the moor and through a pine plantation above Errwood Reservoir. This is Fernilee's younger sibling, completed in 1967 to supplement Stockport's water supply. On the opposite side of the reservoir, a concrete bridge carries the new road, while high above is the long heathery ridge of Shining Tor.

Reaching a four-way junction at a signpost on the old Salt Way (the short-cut back to Goyts Lane car park), cross straight over and follow the path which curves round above a narrow arm of the reservoir. Passing an old lime kiln, where lime was burned for use as fertiliser, you continue up the clough to a bridge made from two iron girders. Don't cross, but carry on up the valley of Wildmoorstone Brook.

Looking across at the 3 routes to Buxton

The path climbs a little, then forking right you stay in the valley near the stream. Wild Moor certainly lives up to its name, for it feels very remote as you follow the deserted valley. Keeping to the lower path, you cross a slatted bridge and beginning to climb, a line of wooden posts leads up the slope until suddenly you arrive at the track of the Cromford and High Peak Railway by the mouth of Burbage Tunnel.

Although the entrance was only bricked up in the 1960s, this part of the line closed in 1892 when more powerful locomotives allowed a new route to be taken. When it was built in 1830, trains needed an almost level track, and the railway was designed like a canal, with steep inclines instead of locks, and stationary engines to haul the wagons up.

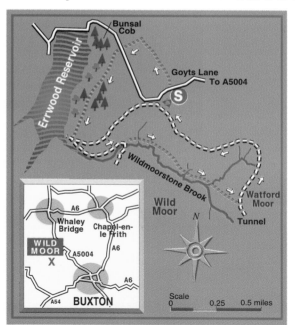

The rest of the walk is completely flat, and turning left you follow the contours around Watford Moor. There are extensive views across the Wildmoorstone Brook valley to Burbage Edge grouse moor, and the track brings you back to Goyts Lane, where the small reservoir provided water for the stationary steam engines.

87

VALUABLE POINTER

Ashurst Beacon

LOCATION: 6 miles west of Wigan

START: Beacon Country Park Visitor Centre, Up Holland, off Mill Lane, toilets

DISTANCE: 3 miles

GRADE: Easy

TIME: 1½ hours

NOTE: Can be muddy

BUS: From Wigan 385

MAP: Pathfinder 711, Landranger 108

REFRESHMENTS: Visitor Centre & Ashurst Beacon Inn

As Napoleon's troops massed across the channel, and all England was expecting invasion, a chain of warning beacons was built across the country. The attack never came, but two centuries later the pyramid spire of Ashurst Beacon still stands high above the Douglas Valley.

There are legacies too of the Civil War, for a farmhouse bears marks where swords were sharpened and holes blasted by gunshot. But now the hilltop is a Country Park, with quiet woods and open meadows, and a spectacular view of the Lancashire lowlands stretching westwards to the sea.

THE ROUTE

From the far end of the car park, follow the path over the little bridge to a striking sculpture, which was carved from the trunk of a 200-year-old chestnut tree. Continuing left through the trees, a path leads to another sculpture, where you turn right on the track and then left beside a belt of woodland. Then as the track bends away, you keep straight on to the road.

Take care crossing Beacon Lane and follow the footpath which wriggles round behind the house. The path keeps to the edge of the field, with the dome and spires of St Joseph's College projecting above the hilltop, while across the wide flat Douglas Valley lie Winter Hill and Anglezarke Moor. The Roman Catholic Seminary, which was built in 1883, is now a Theological Institute.

The path then goes through a narrow strip of woodland by Rough Park Quarry, where the land is being reclaimed. Continuing along the field boundary and beside the golf course, you join Crow Lane at a wooden stile beyond a bungalow.

Turn left up the lane, then at the next bend go right along the farm track. Forking left at the junction, you pass the grand Stone Hall. This was built in the early 18th century, though the stone 'twirls' above the door date from 1640. The sword marks and gunshot holes of the Civil War can be seen on the cornerstone by the drainpipe, but please keep to the path and don't disturb the farmer.

Stone Hall

Continue along the rough track to the bend, where a narrow path goes left down into a little valley, and across a stream. The muddy track climbs on between ancient hedgerows to a wooden stile. Reaching a tarmac track, you go right to Atherton's Farm, then follow the way-marked route round the field edge and out to Long Heyes Lane.

Crossing straight over, follow the field boundary round and above a wooded clough to a footbridge. The path goes left into the next field and stays by the clough to another stile. Forking right through the trees, a path then leads up the steep grassy slope to Ashurst Beacon, a watchtower built by Sir William Ashurst in 1798, where a topograph details the view over seven counties.

A path then leads along the ridge and out to Beacon Lane. Turn left, past the Ashurst Beacon Inn, then cross the road and follow the path down through the trees. Turning left again along the bottom of the bluebell wood, the way-marked path continues through the strip of woodland beside the golf course back to the Visitor Centre.

89

A 20 MILLION HOST...

Swettenham, Daffodil Dell

LOCATION: Between Holmes Chapel & Congleton

START: From A535 at Twemlow, follow signs for Swettenham. Fork right along Congleton Road, then park at third road junction, 1 mile from Swettenham village (Grid ref 810677)

DISTANCE: 6 (or 2) miles

GRADE: Easy, but the longer walk can be muddy and slippery in places

TIME: Allow half a day, but longer if including the arboretum

MAP: Pathfinder 775 & 776, Landranger 118

REFRESHMENTS: Swettenham Arms

Hidden in a maze of narrow country lanes in deepest Cheshire, Daffodil Dell is one of the loveliest sights of spring. Acres of golden blooms cover the wooded slopes above a brook which flows down to the meandering River Dane, while Swettenham village dates back to Anglo-Saxon times. The bulbs have been planted over many years by the Lancaster family, who once worked Swettenham Mill. And how many daffodils are there? They have been counted by the Ministry of Agriculture and Fisheries, so it's official, there are over 20 million!

THE ROUTE

From the road junction, take the footpath which is signed over a stile in the hedge. Heading for the house, the path keeps by the fence, then way-marks point you over stiles and across the drive to continue along the field hedge.

Reaching the tarmac lane, you go left, past an attractive old farm and a Nature Reserve. The unimproved grassland here is full of wildflowers, while in spring there are nests of warblers and whitethroats. Then at Ashtree Farm, the short walk goes left, following the track back into Swettenham village.

The longer route however goes straight on, past Brook Farm, until just before the barns, you turn left over a stile. Skirting the farmyard, the way-marked route continues along the top of the bank, high above Swettenham Brook and the water meadows. Then, after descending to a wooden plank bridge, you climb through a bluebell wood to follow the edge of the trees high above the River Dane.

As the path starts to descend, way-marks indicate a right turn along a belt of Scots pine to a pretty little wooded clough. Heading straight on across the fields, towards the grand 23-arched Twemlow Viaduct which opened in 1842, you come to Macclesfield Road.

Turning left take care! Thankfully, a pavement is reached at the small toll house, and you follow the road uphill. At Saltersford Corner, turn left to follow the hawthorn-hedged tarmac lane, and ahead is a splendid panorama of the Peak District hills. Then passing Woodhouse Farm, the track leads down into the valley and, just after the field gate, a stile on the right leads into Pinfold Rough.

Emerging into the open, Countryside Commission way-marks follow the field edge down to the River Dane and, with the river as a close companion, you follow its meanders until North Wood is reached. Climbing

Swettenham church

steeply through the trees, progress is then briefly all ups and downs until joining a track, you go left.

Crossing the bridge to the strangely named Dragons Cave, the metalled lane leads past the entrance to Quinta Arboretum where Sir Bernard Lovell of Jodrell Bank has planted specimen trees and shrubs. Swettenham's church dates back to the 13th century, and behind it lies the whitewashed Swettenham Arms. Once a nunnery, this was connected to the church by an underground passage.

Opposite the church, a way-marked footpath heads straight across the fields to emerge by the entrance to Swettenham Hall drive. Follow Congleton Road down to the 18th century mill, then after exploring Daffodil Dell, you continue up the hill back to the start.

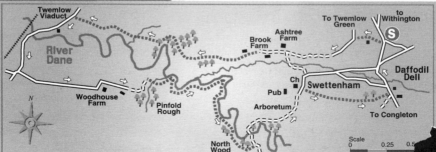

AN EXCEEDINGLY GOOD LAKE

Rudyard Lake

LOCATION: 10 miles south of Macclesfield

START: North end of lake, off A523. Turn right down Beat Lane, then in 200 yards turn left down a rough track. Park where track divides

DISTANCE: 4½ miles

GRADE: Easy

TIME: 2 hours

NOTE: The miniature railway operates most summer weekends

BUS: X1

MAP: Outdoor Leisure - White Peak, Landranger 118

REFRESHMENTS: Hotel Rudyard

Everyone has heard of *The Jungle Book*, but few people realise that its author is named after a Staffordshire lake. Rudyard Kipling's parents were very fond of the area and romantically named their son after the lake beside which they got engaged. The reservoir is edged by attractive woodland, golden plovers nest among the rocks on the shore, sailing boats and fishermen are busy, and there is even a miniature steam railway. But wasn't it lucky that the famous writer's parents came to Rudyard? Just think, Weston-super-Mare Kipling wouldn't have sounded nearly as good!

THE ROUTE

From the car park, take the right fork and follow the track across the feeder channel that brings water from the River Dane. Passing the reed beds at the end of the lake, which are often reduced to mudflats and attract wading birds, the road continues through a gate. The track then swings away from the lake and to the left is a clump of ancient oaks, whose slender trunks and thick boles are the result of frequent coppicing.

At the track junction, fork left along the twin ribbons of tarmac signed with a Staffordshire Knot symbol. This is the way-mark of the Staffordshire Way, a 92 mile long distance path which runs from Mow Cop to Kinver Edge. The track leads to the castellated Cliffe Park Hall, which was built in 1811 at a cost of £20,000. Once a Youth Hostel, there has also been a golf course here. With a marvellous panorama over the lake to the Peak District, you pass in front of the stately hall, which has a grand covered porch and unusual gargoyles on the roof.

An avenue of lime and sycamore trees, nearly 200 years old, leads down to a gate into Rea Cliffe Wood. The track descends gently through the trees to the sailing club, where chalets and boathouses hide among the trees. When the track bends away from the lake, you go left at a wooden signpost.

A little path traverses the bracken slope and continues down a mossy-walled track. After

Rudyard Lake railway

turning uphill past a caravan site, fork left along another old walled path. This descends to join a road which is followed until, just before the Hotel Rudyard car park, a path goes left to the lake.

Rudyard Lake was created to supply the Caldon Canal with water, and below the huge dam

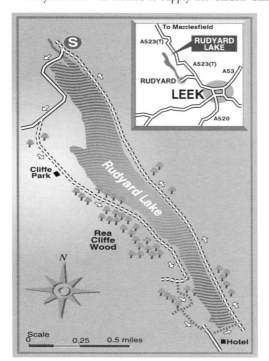

the canal feeder heads off towards Leek. Crossing to the far side, you come to a miniature steam railway which runs along the trackbed of the disused Churnet Valley railway, and if it is working, the next section can be travelled in style.

Turn left along the lake shore to a boathouse, then after climbing up to a picnic area, you join the railway, which was axed in the 1960s. The disused line hugs the lake, where anglers fish for pike, as well as for bream, roach and perch, while in the distance the scarp shape of The Cloud stands out against the sky. Coming to the end of the miniature railway, the broad track continues for another mile until, after passing under a soot-stained railway bridge, you arrive back at the start.

ON ILKLEY MOOR BAHT BATHS

On Ilkley Rocks

LOCATION: 5 miles north of Keighley

START: Ilkley, follow signs to White Wells. Parking on Wells Road, just beyond the cattle grid

DISTANCE: 6 (or 2) miles

GRADE: Moderate, boots recommended for longer walk

TIME: 3 (or 1½) hours

NOTE: White Wells open weekends and when the flag is flying

TRAIN: Ilkley

MAP: Explorer - Lower Wharfedale, Landranger 104

REFRESHMENTS: White Wells

'Tha'll go and get thi deeath o'cowld, on Ilkla Moor baht 'at'. There was a stiff breeze blowing so, heeding the warning of Yorkshire's National Anthem, we wrapped up warmly for the ascent to the Cow and Calf Rocks. High above Ilkley, the views are spectacular, while on the moor lie ancient cup and ring-marked rocks and the mysterious Swastika Stone. And then there is White Wells, where you can take the 'Ilkley Cure', or even attempt to break the 20 minute record for staying in the icy water! But resisting the temptation, we sampled the home-made cakes in the tea room instead.

THE ROUTE

Cross Wells Road and climb to the little shelter, where a path leads above the houses through the heather and bracken. Then joining a good surfaced path, this leads to the Tarn, which was landscaped by the Victorians.

From the far end, a path climbs gently to Backstone Beck, where scattered pines grow in the ravine, then crossing the footbridge you follow the stepped path heading up towards the rocks. On meeting an old track, turn right up to the trees, then just before the quarry, take the left fork which climbs to Cow Rock. The summit is completely covered with Victorian graffiti, while far below is the isolated Calf Rock.

Heading now south west, away from the edge, a path leads to the left of the disused quarry and, crossing Backstone Beck, climbs to the top of Ilkley Crags. This is a marvellous viewpoint with the open moor to the south while northwards, across the natural landslip of Rocky Valley, is Wharfedale.

The path continues along the top, then after passing two large piles of stones, the Short Route forks right to descend beside the plantation to White Wells. Keeping left, the longer

White Wells

route continues across the moor, heading towards the distant East Buck Stones. There are lines of shooting butts, but the red grouse are safe, for the shooting licence has not been renewed.

The Badger Stone, one of several Cup and Ring-marked Rocks on the moor, lies beside a memorial seat near Spicey Gill, then looping across the deep clough you cross the old Keighley Road and continue in the same direction.

Forking right to the wall corner by the prominent Neb Stone, another Cup-marked Rock, the path continues across the hillside, veering away from the wall. Then, at Black Beck, you meet the wall again and going through a gap continue across the moor, until a right fork slants down to two parallel walls.

Follow these down across the fields to join the right of way, and turn right to reach the fenced Swastika Stone, the oldest rock carving in Yorkshire. This mysterious symbol is also found in Sweden, Greece and India. Keep to the lower path, which follows the top edge of the wood to the footbridge, then passing a reservoir, continues along the edge of the moor to a tarmac lane. Cross straight over and follow the little footpath which runs just above the road before contouring across the hillside to join the track up to White Wells.

Though the water at the Bath House, which dates back to 1700, 'is vitalising, animating, resuscitating, exhilarating, enthusing, sustaining, refreshing, invigorating, delightful and delicious to bathe in', a cuppa in the cafe is nicer! It is then a brief descent on a stepped path down to the shelter and back to Wells Road.

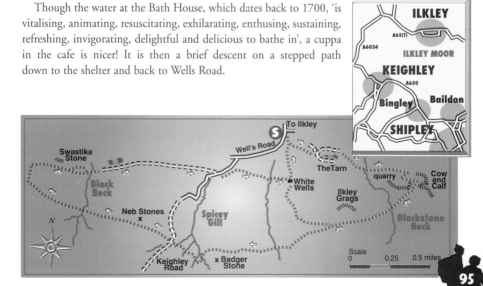

NANCY IN THE SADDLE

White Nancy

LOCATION: 3 miles north east of Macclesfield

START: Middlewood way car park, Adlington Road, Bollington, toilets

DISTANCE: 5½ miles

GRADE: Moderate

TIME: 3 hours

BUS: From Stockport: 392

MAP: Outdoor Leisure - White Peak, Pathfinder 759, Landranger 118

REFRESHMENTS: Redway Tavern

'Here's to the mountain of Nancy, that's built on Ingersley Hill - here's good health, wealth & fancy - & give Dodd another gill'. Mr Dodd, the stonemason, was rightly proud of his white-washed folly which gleams brightly in the sunshine high above the little mill town of Bollington. Built to commemorate the Battle of Waterloo, White Nancy is still a landmark for miles around, and the verse is recorded on the inn sign at Kerridge. So if you pop in, don't forget to raise your glass to Mr Dodd.

THE ROUTE

From the car park, follow the ramp up onto the Bollington Viaduct, and turn left along the disused Macclesfield to Marple railway, which is now the Middlewood Way. On reaching the main road, you go left and up a flight of steps to the Macclesfield Canal. Turning right, the towpath leads past the Adelphi Mill and under the bridge, with a grand view of Kerridge Hill and White Nancy at the northern end. When the quarries on the ridge were in their heyday, a tramway brought down the stone to the Dry Dock where narrowboats now lie moored.

At Clarkes Change Bridge, the towpath crosses to the other side. Then, at Bridge 30, you leave the canal, and a broad track leads across the fields and past some small pools to Moat Hall Farm. Emerging onto Clarke Lane, turn right and at the bend, by the turreted gatehouse of Endon Hall, take the footpath across the fields. The path heads towards Kerridge Hill, then reaching a wall follows it to a stile where you turn right to Swanscoe Farm.

From the house, the farm track leads up to Kerridge Road. Turning left, the climb continues until, reaching Lidgetts Lane, you keep straight on up the rough track past a cottage, and the ridge is reached at the Saddle of Kerridge.

With Rainow far below, go left along the ridge then, after passing through the beech trees, White Nancy comes into view. From the bell-shaped monument there is a bird's eye view of Bollington; to the north-east is Lyme Park, and on a clear day the South Pennine hills can be seen; westwards, beyond Jodrell Bank, the escarpment of Beeston Castle stands out on the Cheshire Plain, and beyond are the Welsh mountains.

Canal by the old dry dock

Trending left, a path leads down to join a track where you go left and down to the Redway Tavern, with its farm animal collection and unusual inn sign. Follow the pavement downhill, then go through the squeezer stile in the stone wall, where a flagged field path leads across the hillside to Woodbank Cottages. Reaching the cobbled lane, a footpath sign almost opposite points you down across the fields. Aim to the right of the house to join a lane where you go left and immediately right on the old quarry tramway.

At a metal fence, the footpath is signed right across the fields to a track. Go left and keep left by the grand gates of Beehive Cottage, then joining the canal, follow the outward route past the Adelphi Mill, but this time stay on the towpath. After Bridge 27, you turn left through the kissing gate and go down Hurst Lane. Cross the main road into the recreation ground, then down to the River Dean and turn left back to the viaduct.

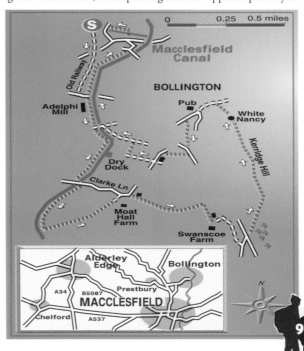

Notes

Public Transport Details

Many of the walks in this guide can easily be reached using buses, trains and Metrolink. When you leave the car at home, the day out starts the minute you leave the house, and you'll be surprised how much more you see when somebody else does the driving. Try the following special tickets…

Rail Ranger: As many train journeys as you wish in Greater Manchester, after 9.30am weekdays and all day weekends and Bank Holidays. £2.45

Evening Ranger: as above, for evenings. £1.25

Day Saver (Bus): Lets you travel on almost any bus in Greater Manchester, no matter which company runs it. Start as early as you like, available from the driver on your first trip. £3

Wayfarer: Allows a day's travel after 9.30am on weekdays and all day weekends and Bank Holidays. Available for almost every bus, train and Metrolink throughout Greater Manchester, parts of Lancashire, Cheshire, Staffordshire and the Peak District. The Wayfarer ticket also allows a discount at many attractions. Must be bought in advance from GMPTE Travelshops, staffed stations and Post Offices. £6.60 (adult), £3.30 (children and OAPs)

For more details, visit a GMPTE Travelshop at bus stations in Greater Manchester, ring the Public Transport Enquiry Bureau on 0161-228 7811 (8am-7pm, every day) or visit the internet journey planner on www.gmpte.gov.uk

Prices shown are correct at August 1999.